Poetry and Experience

Also by Archibald MacLeish

POEMS

Collected Poems, 1917–1952
including Conquistador, Streets in
the Moon, New Found Land, Actfive,
and others
Songs for Eve

PLAYS IN VERSE

Panic
The Fall of the City
Air Raid
The Trojan Horse
This Music Crept by Me upon the Waters
J.B.

PROSE

The Irresponsibles
The American Cause
A Time to Speak
A Time to Act
American Opinion and the War
Poetry and Opinion
Freedom Is the Right to Choose

Poetry and Experience

by Archibald MacLeish

The Riverside Press Cambridge
Houghton Mifflin Company Boston
1 9 6 1

First Printing

Copyright © 1960 by Archibald MacLeish
All rights reserved including the right to
reproduce this book or parts thereof in any form
Library of Congress Catalog Card Number: 60-12742
The Riverside Press
CAMBRIDGE • MASSACHUSETTS
PRINTED IN THE U.S.A.

Grateful acknowledgment is due the following authors and publishers for permission to quote selections from the works cited:

George Allen & Unwin Ltd.: *The White Pony* by Robert Payne.
The John Day Company, Inc.: *The White Pony* by Robert Payne. Copyright © 1947 by The John Day Company. Reprinted by permission of The John Day Company, Inc., publisher.
J. M. Dent & Sons Ltd.: *The Collected Poems of Dylan Thomas.*
Achilles Fang for his translation of Lu Chi's "Wen Fu," first published in the *New Mexico Quarterly.*
Harper & Brothers and Aldous Huxley for the four lines on page 64 of this volume, which are based on Mr. Huxley's translation from the Greek appearing in his book *Texts and Pretexts.*
Harvard University Press: *The Poems of Emily Dickinson,* edited by Thomas H. Johnson. Published by The Belknap Press of Harvard University Press. Copyright 1951, 1955 by The President and Fellows of Harvard College. Reprinted by permission of the publishers.
Alfred A. Knopf, Inc.: *Translations from the Chinese* by Arthur Waley.
Little, Brown & Company: *The Complete Poems of Emily Dickinson,*

To
I. A. Richards
poet
and begetter of poems

Contents

PART I. THE MEANS TO MEANING

Chapter One: Words as Sounds　　3

Chapter Two: Words as Signs　　21

Chapter Three: Images　　43

Chapter Four: Metaphor　　65

PART II. THE SHAPE OF MEANING

Chapter Five: The Private World
Poems of Emily Dickinson　　91

Chapter Six: The Public World
Poems of Yeats　　115

Chapter Seven: The Anti-World
Poems of Rimbaud　　149

Chapter Eight: The Arable World
Poems of Keats　　173

Index　　201

I

The Means
to Meaning

CHAPTER ONE

Words as Sounds

A LION hunt begins with the hypothesis of lion — a roar
in the night — a boy gone or a bullock — an enormous spoor
in the path where the women walk — a fumet out beyond
the thornbushes speculatively examined by the old men.

So with the pursuit of poetry. One begins by assuming
that there is something called poetry to be found.

But whereas one knows in advance what a lion will look
like when one catches up with him, the whole purpose of
the pursuit of poetry is to discover, by running it down,
what a poem is.

The principal difficulty of the undertaking stands therefore
at the outset. The pursuit of poetry must begin more or less
where it hopes to end — with a report of the quarry. And
the danger is precisely there. For if you start with the wrong
report you will end up with the wrong phoenix or the wrong
unicorn — or whatever the fabulous creature turns out to be.

What one needs is a reliable scout, a man who has unques-
tionably been there and come back — which means, of course,

a poet, for the critics, though they have mapped those mountains, have never climbed them themselves.

My own guide for some ten years past has been a Chinese poet and general who was executed in the year 303 of our era for the mistake of losing a battle, but who found time, prior to that definitive event, to write a Fu, a sort of extended prose poem, on literature and specifically on the poet's art. Somehow or other this Fu of Lu Chi's, though long admired by the most famous poets of China, had never succeeded in making its way out of the Celestial Kingdom, and it was not until our own generation that it began to be known among writers in the West. When it became available, however, in translations — and most notably in the translation of my colleague, Achilles Fang — there was immediate recognition of its curious but unquestionable authority. Far more than either Aristotle or Horace, Lu Chi speaks to our condition as contemporary men. Observations which appear at first glance to be no more than clichés of Chinese rhetoric turn out on reflection to convey timely bits of intelligence from beyond the mountains which the pursuit of poetry must cross.

The Fu begins with a modest little explanation in prose of the reasons which led Lu Chi to undertake his ambitious labor. Each time he studies the works of great writers, he says, he flatters himself that he knows how their minds work — a disarming claim which most of us might make ourselves if we were equally candid. But he has his pride too. He is himself a poet. He is hewing his axe handle, as he deftly puts it, with an axe-handle in hand. ". . . what I am able to say," he concludes, "I have put down here."

And the first thing he finds himself able to say is nothing less than how a poem gets itself written:

Taking his position at the hub of things [the poet] contemplates the mystery of the universe;

He feeds his emotions and his mind on the great works
of the past. Moving along with the four seasons, he sighs at
the passing of time;
Gazing at the myriad objects, he thinks of the complex-
ity of the world.
He sorrows over the falling leaves in virile autumn;
He takes joy in the delicate bud of fragrant spring. With
awe at heart he experiences chill;
His spirit solemn, he turns his gaze to the clouds. He
declaims the superb works of his predecessors;
He croons the clean fragrance of past worthies. He roams
in the forest of literature, and praises the symmetry of
great art. Moved, he pushes his books away and takes the
writing brush, that he may express himself in letters.

Now, obviously, much of this is rhetoric, and conventional
at that, but there is also something that is not rhetorical and
not conventional. This account, deceptive in its seeming
simplicity, of the way in which a poem comes about, provides
also a hint, a suggestion, of what a poem is — how it would
look if you ran it to earth out in that wilderness where it
exists and where every man is alone.

The usual notion of the way in which a poem gets itself
written — usual in the West at least — is the one on which
we were all brought up. The man about to be poet is a
man lost in himself. He is not capable of outward vision but
only of inward — an "eye in a fine frenzy rolling" doesn't
see. He is a solipsist, a candle flame consuming its own fat, a
pearl diver emerging blind and breathless from the ocean of
himself. This is the traditional conception and it is also the
conception favored by those of our contemporaries who re-
gard themselves as most contemporaneous. Sir Herbert Read
has spoken of modern man in the act of art as awaiting
"some symbol rising unaided from the depths of his uncon-
scious."

And, of course, to think of the writing of a poem in this way is to think in the same way of the nature of poetry. If the act of art is a passive waiting for the symbol to emerge from the depths of the unconscious, then a poem is a secret and isolated event, a rhapsodic cry, something heard at dark far off like that nightingale of the famous ode.

There are many who think just this of the art of poetry — many who think in consequence that even the attempt at pursuit is foolish or worse. But Lu Chi, as you will have noticed, is not one of them. To Lu Chi the begetting of a poem involves not a single electric pole thrust deep into the acids of the self but a pair of poles — a man and the world opposite. A poem begins, in the Wen Fu, not in isolation but in relationship. There is the writer here. And over there, there is "the mystery of the universe" — the "four seasons" — "the myriad objects" — "the complexity of the world." Instead of the symbol arising like Venus of her own motion from the sea there is an image, a poem, achieved in the space *between* — that space we all look out on — the space between ourselves on the one side and the world on the other. And finally instead of the attentive watcher and waiter brooding above the silence of himself, there is a man "taking" a position — "his position" . . . where? "At the hub of things."

It is a teasing phrase. There is a sense in which we are all of us always at the hub of things for we seem to ourselves to exist at the unturning center of our turning experience. But Lu Chi obviously means something more and something different. His position at the hub of things is a position a man *takes* explicitly and for a purpose: to face "the mystery of the universe," to face the world, to see the world. It is from this hub of things that the myriad objects are visible — those myriad objects that most of us stare at all our lives and never see. It is from this hub that the complexity of the world, that complexity which most of us succeed so easily in ignoring, can be observed. It is at this hub that the irresistible sweep of time, that tide which most of us take for granted and so never feel until it has all but carried us away, is felt as movement. Lu Chi's hub, in brief, is not a spatial center, such as the one illusion tells us we occupy, but a center of awareness, a center of receptivity. It is a position much like the position Keats describes in that famous sentence of his about what he calls "negative capability," the capability he says Shakespeare had to live in "uncertainty, mystery and doubt" without any irritable reaching after fact and reason: without, that is to say, struggling to scramble ashore out of swirling, buffeting awareness of world, to those dry sandpits of "fact" and "reason" which keep the ocean off and so make seeming refuges for our minds.

Now it is obvious that this account of the process is also an account, or the beginning of an account, of the nature of the art. If a poem gets itself written, not in a rhapsodic cry but in a relationship of man and world, then poetry is something which has to do with that relationship — something which *traffics* in some way between world and man. But in what way? Lu Chi tells us. The poet is one who "traps Heaven and Earth in the cage of form." He is not, in other words, that inventor of free forms of whom we like to think — that exuberant fountain. On the contrary, he is a hunter and trapper to whom form is a net used for a bold and serious purpose, a purpose not without risk: to cage, to capture, the whole of experience, experience *as* a whole — heaven and earth. Capture it how? Well, what is "form" in art? Is it not meaningful shape? — shape which the senses recognize as meaningful whatever the mind can say? — shape to which the emotions answer?

What Lu Chi is saying with that urbane smile is something,

therefore, we had not altogether expected: something indeed quite unexpected. He is saying that the poet's art is a *means to meaning* — a means by which the world can be made to mean. Now, we are accustomed, of course, to talk about meaning. We are accustomed to the notion that philosophy can make the world mean and that science can discover meaning in it. But we have not heard this claim made for poetry, which we have been taught to think of as inhabiting a world of its own. And above all, we have not been prepared for this calm assumption of Lu Chi's, which goes beyond the claims made for either science or philosophy. For philosophy has never pretended to do more than substitute for the meaningless complexities of world an organization of abstractions which, read in abstract terms, is meaningful. And science discovers meaning, not in stones or chairs or tables or the stars themselves, but in those fabulous equations which contain the stars, those "laws" which can account for chairs and tables. Not so the poem as Lu Chi conceives it. Lu Chi's poem *captures whole*. It cages the world with all its complexities upon it. It takes experience as experience stands there. It closes the cage of form on heaven and earth and makes them *mean* — makes them mean not in other terms but in their own.

That Lu Chi intended the implications of his metaphor cannot be questioned. Later in the Fu you find these coupled sentences:

> We poets struggle with Non-being to force it to yield Being;
>   We knock upon silence for an answering music.
>
> We enclose boundless space in a square foot of paper;
>   We pour out deluge from the inch space of the heart.

Consider what this means. The "Being" which the poem is to contain derives from "Non-being," not from the poet. And the "music" which the poem is to own comes not from us who make the poem but from the silence: comes in *answer* to our knock. The verbs are eloquent: "struggle," "force," "knock." The poet's labor is not to wait until the cry gathers of itself in his own throat. The poet's labor is to struggle with the meaninglessness and silence of the world until he can force it to mean: until he can make the silence answer and the non-Being BE. It is a labor which undertakes to "know" the world not by exegesis or demonstration or proofs but directly, as a man knows apple in the mouth.

In a course I have been teaching — or rather, in which I have been taught — a course out of which this book has emerged — I have suggested to my students that they accept this report brought back fifteen hundred years ago by the unhappy poet and general at least until they can replace it by an account of the art they find more persuasive. But to accept this description of the nature of the art even tentatively is to accept also an obligation to answer certain difficult questions. How, for example, is it possible, by any means of meaning, to carry world across into mind *whole* in all its complexities? How can boundless space actually be enclosed in a square foot of paper? That it can be we have not only Lu Chi's assertion but Dante's *Comedy* to attest, and yet — how can it? And how can deluge pour from the inch space of the heart? Rimbaud has done it but how has it been done?

Precisely how difficult these questions are I think I know. I do not however agree with those who maintain that they are questions too difficult to answer or even to discuss. Poems are made by men and if men cannot undertake to comprehend their making, then poems are smaller not greater, weaker not stronger, on that account. Anyone, I submit, who will begin, not with talk about poetry but with poetry itself, can make his way to conclusions of a kind and even, conceivably, to conclusions he can accept as true.

Begin, therefore, with a poem — borrow an axe-handle as a pattern for the axe-handle you are about to attempt to hew. The poem I should suggest is one not only famous in itself but famous in the author's reading of it, for the author was, in my judgment at least, the finest reader of his own work of whom we have record: Dylan Thomas's "Do Not Go Gentle Into That Good Night."

> *Do not go gentle into that good night,*
> *Old age should burn and rave at close of day;*
> *Rage, rage against the dying of the light.*
>
> *Though wise men at their end know dark is right,*
> *Because their words have forked no lightning they*
> *Do not go gentle into that good night.*
>
> *Good men, the last wave by, crying how bright*
> *Their frail deeds might have danced in a green bay,*
> *Rage, rage against the dying of the light.*
>
> *Wild men who caught and sang the sun in flight,*
> *And learn, too late, they grieved it on its way,*
> *Do not go gentle into that good night.*
>
> *Grave men, near death, who see with blinding sight*
> *Blind eyes could blaze like meteors and be gay,*
> *Rage, rage against the dying of the light.*
>
> *And you, my father, there on the sad height,*
> *Curse, bless, me now with your fierce tears, I pray.*
> *Do not go gentle into that good night.*
> *Rage, rage against the dying of the light.*

I think we can probably agree that this poem is a trap and cage in which a heaven and earth we recognize is somehow caught. A boy's agony, face to face with the humility and submission of a dying father, is held here in such a way that we not only know the pain but know also something we had not known before about that mysterious turning away which is the cause of pain. But can we go further still? Can we say *how* this knowing is given to us?

We can take, I think, at least one step. We can agree that whatever it is we know in this poem, we know only *in* the poem. It is not a knowledge we can extract from the poem like a meat from a nut and carry off. It is something the *poem* means — something that is gone when the poem goes and recovered only by returning to the poem's words. And not only by returning to the poem's words but by returning to them within the poem. If we alter them, if we change their order, though leaving their sense much as it is, if we speak them so that their movement changes, their meaning changes also.

This far, we can surely go together, for the simplest experiment will prove these statements true. But can we go beyond this? Can we say how it is that these words in this order and moving to this movement have the power to contain a meaning which can so easily be lost and which cannot elsewhere be found? These words of Dylan Thomas's are very ordinary words — in no way remarkable. They are grouped in simple sentences. There is nothing unusual about them in any way — nothing fantastic or violent or particularly memorable even. And yet we know what they can do because they have done it. What explanation can we give ourselves?

Well, there is a question we can ask which will perhaps give us a direction in which to look. Simple and familiar as they are, is there nothing unusual about these words as words-in-the-poem? Are they in no way different there from the same words in a paragraph of prose — in no way different from the same words arranged in the order and pattern of a paragraph of prose? Obviously, as I think you will agree, they are different. They seem to have what I can only call, for myself, more *weight* than the same words have when we run across them in ordinary conversation or on the page of a newspaper or even on a page of prose. There is an enhancement of their meanings or perhaps, more precisely, of the significance of their meanings. It is not an enhancement which can be defined by abstract analysis and measurement. But the inability to define in abstract terms does not mean, contrary to notions now in vogue, that an experience is fanciful. It is still possible, even under the new vocabulary, to feel as well as to define. And what is present here is *felt*.

The words of the poem have — have inescapably when placed in the poem and in the author's voicing of the poem — a sense of signifying something "more" — the kind of look a familiar face may have when head turns, eyes meet, in an unexpected way — the kind of look a familiar landscape takes on in a sidewise light. This "rage" of Dylan's is not the rage one sees in a child in tantrums or a mother crossed or even in an Alexander in a play. This "dying of the light" is not a mere diminishment at evening. This "good night" is neither "good" nor "night" nor yet a simple saying of farewell but all of them together and much more than all. Emotion *knows* the difference even though mind is defeated in its busy effort to pinch the difference between the thumb and finger of reason and so dispose of it. Emotion — and this is perhaps the point precisely — cannot dispose of it. Emotion stands there staring.

Ezra Pound has a wonderful phrase about good writing which, because Pound is a poet, is really applicable to poetry alone. He talks about each and every word being "charged with meaning." That is what has happened here. These words are charged with meaning in the poem as they are not charged with meaning outside it. Or rather they are charged, in the poem, with a particular kind of meaning: a meaning which goes straight to what we call the heart — intending by that term the organ of intelligence which takes its meanings whole and live, not masticated into chewed abstractions. But how are they so charged? Or is this the question one cannot ask, because it is the question which attempts to pick the lock of the secret of the creative act? Or can we ask it? Can we ask it in humility and patience, leaving the poem to reply?

Return for a moment and read the simple words of the poem again. Read them simply, letting them take their sure positions within the structure which contains them. You will see — have already seen — what some of the formal relationships are. They are very obvious. They can even be stated in statistical terms. For one thing, the words are arranged in a grammatical order as words are in ordinary compositions. Here, there are eight sentences, each of them simple in form — imperative or declarative. But it is not only these sentences which hold the words together. They are also held in another kind of structure: a structure the elements of which have nothing to do with sentences or syntax but with something which sentences and syntax regard as irrelevant and fortuitous — the *sounds* the words make in the mouth and in the ear when they are spoken — the accenting or unaccenting of their syllables — the sounds of their letters, both consonants and vowels. They are arranged, first of all, in "lines," nineteen in all, each "line" consisting of ten syllables, five accented and five not. These "lines," in turn, are so arranged that they end in words which, as we say, "rhyme." The rhymes, again, are two in number based on "night" and "day," the first rhyme appearing thirteen times and the second six, in a regular pattern. Finally — though this does not exhaust the elements of construction — two of the lines are repeated four times each. These statistics may be impertinent and annoying but the structure they describe is obviously neither. It is a structure deliberately and purposefully composed of words as sounds, or, more precisely, of the repetitions of words as sounds. Now the question is: Is there a relationship between this structure and the capacity of the poem to mean? — the capacity of the words to mean more than their ordinary meanings?

Manifestly there is. I say manifestly because it is only this structure which distinguishes the relationships of these familiar words in their familiar order from their usual relationships in the sentences and syntax of prose. But does it follow — and this is, of course, the essential question — does it follow that it is *because* and solely because of the structure of the words as sounds that the meaning of the words as meanings is enhanced? One of the greatest poets of the last century and one of the most intellectually precise and articulate minds of many centuries apparently thought so. Writing to Degas in a famous letter Stéphane Mallarmé gave it as his flat and considered opinion that poetry is made not with ideas but with words. Since ideas are expressed in words and cannot very well exist without them, and since many words signify ideas whether we wish them to or not, this statement must be taken to mean that poetry is made not with words-as-expressions-of-ideas but with what Mallarmé elsewhere called "words themselves," words as sensuous events — in brief, words as the sounds that convey them.

What this assertion comes down to then — the assertion that poetry is made not with "ideas" but with "words" — what it comes down to is the proposition that it is exclusively in the relationships of words as sounds that the poem as poem exists. The poem's meaning is evoked by the structure of words-as-sounds rather than by the structure of words-as-meanings. And the enhancement of meaning, which we feel in any true poem, is a product, therefore, of the structure of the sounds.

You will permit me, perhaps, to observe in passing that Mallarmé's position, extreme though it may appear, is no more extreme in its way than a contrary notion which has gained acceptance in contemporary intellectual circles and which can even be encountered in the university — the notion that words may be so used as to be stripped clean of every association and effect *except* their "meanings," thus becoming intellectual symbols as precise and as sterilized as the symbols of the mathematicians. I have heard loving homage paid to these imaginary words which are described as "hard" and "clean" — both adjectives, you will notice, being metaphors with rich and shadowy implications about their shoulders — and I have never failed to think of Mallarmé when the ritual phrases start.

But to return to our sounds and to our question. Is it in fact true that the answer is as clear as Mallarmé's Gallic clarity makes it seem? Is it a fact of experience that poetry is made with "words themselves"? Is the meaning of the words of a poem — the enhancement of meaning which all right readers of poetry have encountered — an incident, a consequence, of the relations of their sounds? *Can* words be picked up by their sounds? And if they can be picked up by their sounds will their meanings still follow them? And if their meanings do follow their sounds will their meanings thus be enhanced?

There are certain words, as we all know, which *can* be picked up by their sounds. The sound of buzz is the meaning of buzz. The sound of bark is the meaning of bark.

And so it goes through the whole range of onomatopoetic words. The sound means.

There are also combinations of words which sound their meanings even though their meanings may ooze out a little beyond the sound. Tennyson's "murmur of innumerable bees" is the stock example.

Then again there are many words in which the sound implies the meaning not in a direct equivalence but by a detour of some kind through the associative habits of the mind. *Numbness* as a sensation has no sound, but the sound of the word *numb* is "like" it. And so of a number of words having the same combination of letters. A wall that doesn't really fall *crumbles*. A man who doesn't quite go down *stumbles*. A mouth that lacks the courage to speak out *mumbles*. There is an implication of impotence in the letters themselves as we hear them in the ear.

But beyond these classes of words and others like them, how many words are there in which the sound of the word *signifies?* Are there, as certain critics have suggested, "bright" and "dark" vowels — "harsh" and "tender" consonants? I find it hard to believe and I can find little evidence in actual poems that the poets believed it either.

But a better way, perhaps, of approaching the problem is to turn to the work of the writer who has gone farthest in the effort to manipulate the sounds of words with a view to enriching their meanings. I mean, of course, James Joyce in *Finnegans Wake*. Here is a passage from the most widely quoted section of that book:

> Well, you know or don't you kennet or haven't I told you every telling has a taling and that's the he and the she of it. Look, look, the dusk is growing! My branches lofty are taking root. And my cold cher's gone ashley. Fieluhr?

Filou! What age is at? It saon is late. 'Tis endless now
senne eye or erewone last saw Waterhouse's clogh. They
took it asunder, I hurd thum sigh. When will they reassem-
ble it? O, my back, my back, my bach! I'd want to go to
Aches-les-Pains. Pingpong! There's the Belle for Sexaloi-
tez! And Concepta de Send-us-pray! Pang! Wring out the
clothes! Wring in the dew! Godavari, vert the showers! And
grant thaya grace! Aman. Will we spread them here now?
Ay, we will. Flip! Spread on your bank and I'll spread mine
on mine. Flep! It's what I'm doing. Spread! It's churning
chill. Der went is rising. I'll lay a few stones on the hostel
sheets. A man and his bride embraced between them. Else
I'd have sprinkled and folded them only. And I'll tie my
butcher's apron here. It's suety yet. The strollers will pass
it by. Six shifts, ten kerchiefs, nine to hold to the fire and
this for the code, the convent napkins, twelve, one baby's
shawl. Good mother Jossiph knows, she said. Whose head?
Mutter snores? Deataceas! Wharnow are alle her childer,
say? In kingdome gone or power to come or gloria be to
them farther? Allalivial, allalluvial! Some here, more no
more, more again lost alla stranger. I've heard tell that same
brooch of the Shannons was married into a family in Spain.
And all the Dunders de Dunnes in Markland's Vineland
beyond Brendan's herring pool takes number nine in yang-
see's hats. And one of Biddy's beads went bobbing till she
rounded up lost histereve with a marigold and a cobbler's
candle in a side strain of a main drain of a manzinahurries
off Bachelor's Walk. But all that's left to the last of the
Meaghers in the loup of the years prefixed and between is
one kneebuckle and two hooks in the front. Do you tell
me that now? I do in troth. Orara por Orbe and poor
Las Animas! Ussa, Ulla, we're umbas all! Mezha, didn't
you hear it a deluge of times, ufer and ufer, respund to
spond? You deed, you deed! I need, I need! It's that
irrawaddyng I've stoke in my aars. It all but husheth
the lethest zswound . . .

No one else, I think, has assumed as explicitly as Joyce did that words as sounds are malleable and may be made to multiply their meanings by the management of their shapes and movements in the ear. When Joyce was told that *Finnegans Wake* was unintelligible he always replied in the same way: "Read it aloud!" "Listen to it!" And if you have the chance to listen to it — to compare the printed page of it with a few minutes of one of the recorded readings by an accomplished actress like Siobhan McKenna, or by the master himself, I think you will agree that *Finnegans Wake* is, as Joyce said it would be, more intelligible to the ear than it is to the eye — which, if true, implies that it is the management of the sounds which works in it to distort and multiply the meanings. But I hazard the guess that you would agree to something else also: to the proposition that the margin of manipulation is narrow — that there is an obvious limiting principle — the same principle which limits the manufacture of puns. You can go no farther in the mixing of word with word in the making of puns than the recognizability of the elements combined will let you. And the same thing remained true for Joyce: he could alter the sounds of words no farther than the sense would follow.

The conclusion I should reach would be something like this: that the sounds of words are obviously not *the* plastic material of the art of poetry as stone is the plastic material of the art of sculpture. Those caryatids on the Acropolis are made of blocks of marble which had never been girls before, but any sound which makes a word has meant the meaning of that word for centuries past and can't be used in a poem without so meaning. To lose the meaning you must lose the word. If you want the sound of *lurk* instead of the sound of *lark* in your sonnet you can write it down but your bird will disappear. If you want to play sonorous games with *l'amour, la mort* and *la mer* you may: but you will still have love, death and the sea on your hands with no possibility of escape — except perhaps to Mother.

It would follow that it cannot be the management of the sounds *alone* which produces the enhancement of meaning which words in a poem gain. The *meanings* of the sounds are also present and cannot help but play a part. I should like now to consider what that part is and how it relates to the part played by the management of the sounds. Are the meanings also managed in some more-than-usually *formal* way? And if they are is it in that management that the answer lies or in a relation — but what relation? — between the management of meanings and the management of sounds? With these questions in the air let me return for a moment to Joyce.

When James Joyce wrote poems, he did not write them in the dissolving language of *Finnegans Wake*. Joyceans will protest that his poems were written earlier before the great liberation had taken place. I can only reply that Joyce gave me my copy of *Pomes Penyeach* in the same summer in which he read me the Anna Livia fragment I have quoted. There was no question in my mind then — and there seems to be no question in the mind of Joyce's fine biographer, Richard Ellmann, now — that he cared a great deal, even on the sixth of July, 1927, what the reader of those poems thought of them. Consider the sounds of the words in "On the Beach at Fontana":

> *Wind whines and whines the shingle,*
> *The crazy pierstakes groan;*
> *A senile sea numbers each single*
> *Slimesilvered stone.*
>
> *From whining wind and colder*
> *Grey sea I wrap him warm*
> *And touch his trembling fineboned shoulder*
> *And boyish arm.*

Around us fear, descending
Darkness of fear above
And in my heart how deep unending
Ache of love!

CHAPTER TWO

Words as Signs

MALLARMÉ, who insisted that poetry is made out of "words themselves," meaning words as sensuous events, was not alone in rejecting ideas as the stuff of poetry. The Irish writer George Moore had the same notion a few decades later: "pure poetry," he said, is poetry "unsicklied o'er with the pale cast of thought," and he proposed to make an anthology to prove it. But it was not of "words themselves" that Moore's poems were to be made, but of words as signifiers of "things." In his anthology the words of a poem were to be allowed to "mean" but only within limits — only if they meant "things" perceived in detachment "from the personality of the poet" — only if they meant "things" seen in "innocency of vision" — "things" seen as themselves without the intrusion of the poet's thoughts *about* them.

George Moore was, of course, no poet, and this recipe shows why. A poet goes to the "things" of the world not to have thoughts *about* them but to discover them and so to discover himself looking at them. It is a prose writer's

mistake to suppose that a man writes poems in order to ex-
press thoughts and that the "things" he notices are noticed
for the thought's sake. Lu Chi knew better 1500 years ago.
But Moore's anthology is interesting nevertheless for the
light it throws, however unintentionally, on the question
which concerns us here — the question of the way in which
poems mean — their means to meaning. Granted that poems
are made of words, in what way are they made of words?
Not, I think we agree, of words used only as sounds. The
meaning stubbornly inheres. But how then are the words as
meanings involved in the poem? Merely as in any other use
of words? Any meaning? All meanings? Moore says, No.
Only certain meanings are admissible. If a word-as-meaning
is to find a place in a "pure poem" — which would seem
to say, in "poetry itself" — it must do no more than point
at an object out there on the circumference. But in terms of
Mallarmé's letter to Degas, this comes down to saying:
"Poetry is not made with ideas: it is made with things or
words that signify things."

Is it? Unlike other theories of this kind, Moore's is ac-
companied by the means of testing it. His anthology exists
— exists handsomely and elegantly. It is composed, as
you might expect, of Shakespeare's songs, of lyrics by Poe
and Landor and Tennyson and Swinburne, and of poems by
Shelley — "The Cloud" but not, of course, "Ode to the West
Wind." They are true and beautiful poems and chosen with
discrimination and taste but they do not, to me at least,
demonstrate the truth of the theory they are alleged to il-
lustrate. Consider some lines from three of his selections.
Shakespeare's song which begins:

> *When daisies pied and violets blue*
> *And lady-smocks all silver white*
> *And cuckoo buds of yellow hue*

Do paint the meadows with delight,
The cuckoo then in every tree
Mocks married men; for thus sings he:
                Cuckoo;
Cuckoo, cuckoo: O word of fear,
Unpleasing to a married ear!

Herrick's "To Meadows" which begins:

    Ye have been fresh and green,
      Ye have been fill'd with flowers:
    And ye the walks have been
      Where maids have spent their hours.

Webster's "Dirge" which begins:

    Call for the robin redbreast and the wren,
    Since oer shady groves they hover,
    And, with leaves and flowers, do cover
    The friendless bodies of unburied men.

It is easy in all three to see what part the sound plays. It is easy to see that in all three the words are present as something more than sounds — that they also signify. But is it plain that the meanings of the words in all three are merely the "things" to which they refer? Is it only because they mean these "things" that they are meaningful? If it is, how are we to account for the difference of meanings between them when the "things" to which all three refer are substantially the same — flowers and birds, grass and flowers? Is it only because their patterns of sound are different that they face in opposite directions?

Moore is obviously on the wrong track and it is not too difficult to see how he got there. Anyone who defines art in negatives is lost before he begins. It is not by what it *cannot* do but by what it *does* that poetry is recognized, and the man who declares that a poem is something which does *not* do this or that may live to find himself a fool — or die to bequeath the discovery to others. Ten years before the publication of *Pure Poetry* a compatriot of Moore's, a minor Irish poet named William Butler Yeats, had begun to make himself the greatest poet of his world by doing precisely what Moore declares true poetry cannot do — by using words with all their meanings round them, thoughts as well as things.

No, it is not by discovering laws that one discovers the paths to Parnassus. And certainly it is not by admitting certain meanings of words to the garden of the Muses and excluding others that one discovers how a poem means. There is only one decent and respectful approach to the puzzles of poetry and that is by way of poems.

Mallarmé, whose letter to Degas triggered this discussion of the language of poetry, wrote on another occasion[1] of one of his poems: "This sonnet . . . is inverse, I mean that the sense (if it has one . . .) is evoked by an internal mirage of the words themselves." The poem, that is to say, is made of words as sensuous events, and any meaning these "words-themselves" may have is either accidental or irrelevant or perhaps both — a mirage reflected from the surface of the "words-themselves," a rainbow hanging over them. With these observations in mind let us turn to a sonnet of Mallarmé's — not the one to which his letter refers but another, composed in much the same way:

Le vierge, le vivace et le bel aujourd'hui
Va-t-il nous déchirer avec un coup d'aile ivre

[1] Letter to Henri Cazalis, July 18, 1868. Quoted by Elizabeth Sewell in her *Structure of Poetry* (Scribners', 1952), p. 154.

Ce lac dur oublié que hante sous le givre
Le transparent glacier des vols qui n'ont pas fui!

Un cygne d'autrefois se souvient que c'est lui
Magnifique mais qui sans espoir se délivre
Pour n'avoir pas chanté la région où vivre
Quand du stérile hiver a resplendi l'ennui.

Tout son col secouera cette blanche agonie
Par l'espace infligée à l'oiseau qui le nie,
Mais non l'horreur du sol où le plumage est pris.

Fantôme qu'à ce lieu son pur éclat assigne,
Il s'immobilise au songe froid de mépris
Que vêt parmi l'exil inutile le Cygne.

Perhaps the reader with no fluency in French, who must have the poem read to him if he is to "hear" it at all, would be the best able to receive the "words themselves," for themselves, as they take their pure shape in the ear. That the shape is formal, polished, elegant — in fact beautiful, no one who can hear it will deny. This is the classic French sonnet with the closely contrived classical rhyme scheme, the division into octave and sestet, those two great strophes, and the total wholeness which the fourteen lines, for aesthetic reasons not yet explained by science, seem somehow to give in most Western languages. One descends with reluctance from these lovely sounds to the deliberate harshness of a literal paraphrase, but we must do what we can, and it is the structure of the meanings we are now to be concerned with.

The virgin, the hardy, the beautiful today —
will it tear for us, with one drunken slash of its wing,
this hard forgotten lake haunted under the frost
by the transparent glacier of flights never flown?

A swan of another time remembers: this is himself:
magnificent, but escaping without hope
because he has sung no praise to the place life can keep
when sterile winter has spread its resplendent tedium.

His whole neck will shake off that white agony
inflicted by space on the space-denying bird
but not the horror of earth where his feathers are caught.

Phantom, assigning his pure brilliance to this place,
he stiffens himself to the cold dream of contempt
which amid a useless exile clothes the swan.

Now this, precisely because it is ugly, is *merely* meanings
— the rags and bones of meanings. But it will serve, I think,
to ask the question. Is there, within or in some other as-
sociation with the lovely structure of the sounds, a structure
of meanings? And if there is, *is* it properly described as
a mirage — an internal mirage — of the structure of sounds?

To begin with, we can agree that there is, if not a structure
of meaning, at least a *subject* of meaning. There is a swan
who enters the sonnet in its fifth line and who dominates it
thereafter. There is a frozen lake which serves as antagonist
to the swan. And there is a good fairy or the hope of one —
a lovely, vigorous, virgin *today* which may perhaps — but
will it? — shatter the ice. Ordinarily when a composition
has a subject, an antagonist, and a possible intervener for
good or ill, one would say that there was a structure of
meanings. And there is something else here that one would
ordinarily describe as meaningful. There is a hint that this
swan is not only swan. He is described as a phantom com-
mitted to this place by his own brightness — as immobilized
in a cold dream of contempt — as living in a useless exile.
His whole neck, it is said, will shake off the white agony

inflicted by space on the bird who denies space — but will not shake off the horror of the stain of earth on his plumage. And the frozen lake too seems perhaps to mean more than frozen lake, for it is haunted under the frost by flights which have not flown — by a neglect or denial of flight — by that neglect of flight which is treason in a swan — that neglect which space, the element of flight, has here revenged with this white agony.

Hints of a shape of meaning loom as one moves among these sayings much as hints of a landfall loom in a Maine fog. Frozen lake haunted beneath the frost. A swan — a swan of other days — what was, in other days, a swan — caught in this white (frozen) agony inflicted by space — unable to shake off the horror of the stain of earth from his plumage — remembering that it was he who failed to sing the region where life is possible even in the shining boredom of sterile winter — and now this new day, virgin, alive, lovely — is it going to tear this hard forgotten lake with a stroke of its drunken wing? This is not Baudelaire's albatross — poet whose gigantic wings prevent him from walking — but neither is it a wholly different creature in a wholly different disgrace. One begins to *conceive* this swan frozen into the white ice and the black mire at the pond's edge — to find relationship among the seemingly unrelated meanings of these words.

But how does this relationship of the meanings of the words relate to that other structure — to the order and logic and precision of those same words as sounds? Obviously it does not relate in the usual sense. Here there is no order and no logic. "Today" has a drunken wing which can tear a hard forgotten lake. Flights which haven't flown are a transparent glacier. Swans of other days remember songs they have not sung. Tenses suggest present and future but without present cause or future consequence. And the shape of total meaning when it begins to appear is a shape not in the understanding mind but in the recognizing perceptions — those fingers which can *feel*. There is vivid, immediate, lovely drunken hope here, and there is impotence and despair; that "right reader" Robert Frost has spoken of, will take his "immortal wound"; but there is nothing the mind can *understand* as the ear understands that pattern of equal lines and of rhymes in repetition. Where the structure of sounds is orderly and precise the structure of meanings is neither. The one can be examined, analyzed, counted out, discussed in endless pages of prosodic criticism. The other cannot be analyzed, has nothing to count and measure, and will disappear altogether if it is logically rearranged. But nevertheless and notwithstanding, there is a structure of meaning and it is, to me at least, not an accident or a mirage. On the contrary it is as subtly controlled in one way as the structure of sounds is controlled in another. Indeed, if anything, the control of this strange structure of meanings is more remarkable than the control of the "words themselves," for what is "meant" in this poem is something which is not quite *sayable*, and yet has it not been said?

Mallarmé is entitled, of course, to his own account of his own sonnets. If he prefers to call the sense an internal mirage of the sound, mirage it shall be, but whatever the term, the essential fact will remain — that the structure of words as meanings does not *correspond* in this poem to the structure of the words as sounds. You many say with the great French poet that the one is a more or less fortuitous consequence of the other, or you may say that one is constructed one way and the other otherwise, but in either case you will be saying that the two structures are different.

How *can* they be different? How can the same words

in the same positions and the same order carry two wholly different constructions on their shoulders? For a simple and entirely obvious reason which most of us take so completely for granted that we forget it. Words are *themselves* double constructions.[2] They are sounds which are also signs for meanings and signs for meanings which are also sounds. You cannot use them in one way without using them in the other. You cannot, that is to say, use the sound without the meaning nor can you, as I pointed out in the last chapter, alter the sound materially without altering, or more likely losing, the meaning. Furthermore — as we have also seen — the relation between sound and meaning in most words is purely arbitrary. There is no reason in reason why the sound "love" should mean what it does. The result is that if words are put together as raw material of art to produce patterns of sound, the order that patterns them in the ear will not produce an identical pattern in whatever faculty it is that "understands." On the contrary it will almost certainly produce a different and perhaps discordant pattern and even, if attention is paid to the sound alone, an entire absence of pattern. Swinburne, when he lets his fingers improvise on the keyboard of his mellifluous vocabulary, often means nothing at all.

The double structure of poetry, in other words, is not a modern invention: something Mallarmé conceived for his dense and difficult descendents to imitate. It is an inevitable consequence of the use of language as material of art. No poet has ever been able to avoid or evade it and every reader of poetry has been subject to it whether he was aware of it or not. Even those who hold to the thought-

[2] Ogden and Richards consider words from this point of view in *The Meaning of Meaning* and Miss Elizabeth Sewell has a critical discussion of the problem and the relevant literature in her *Structure of Poetry*.

less notion that sound in poetry is mere embellishment or mere "music" are at least conscious — faintly and numbly conscious — of the fact that the structure of sound and the structure of sense are not the same.

But if they are not the same, in what way are they different? If the structure of sound is an orderly structure composed of repetitions and intervals — a structure which the reason can analyze and understand — what is the structure of meanings which these same words in this same order must, because they are words, produce? Is it possible to say? Is it possible, that is, to make a general statement of any value when the sense of each true poem differs so uniquely from the sense of every other? Poems can be grouped by the structure of their sounds as, for example, sonnets or quatrains or poems in what used to be called "free verse." But true poems cannot be grouped, despite the best efforts of the anthologists, by the structure of their meanings, let alone by their actual sense. What general statement, then, is possible?

With this question in mind, let us look at a few familiar lyric poems which would certainly defy easy grouping: an early and anonymous English lyric, a sonnet of Shakespeare's, a lyric of Herrick's, and one of the most characteristic of "modern" poems, a section of Pound's "Hugh Selwyn Mauberley."

Let us begin with the anonymous lyric:

> *The maidens came*
> *When I was in my mother's bower.*
> *I had all that I wolde.*
> *The baily berith the bell away;*
> *The lilly, the rose, the rose I lay.*
>
> *The silver is whit, red is the golde;*
> *The robes they lay in fold.*

The baily berith the bell away;
The lilly, the rose, the rose I lay.

And through the glasse window shines the sone.
How should I love and I so young?
The baily berith the bell away;
The lilly, the rose, the rose I lay.

Here the structure of meanings is ostensibly simple and obvious — a series of statements. The maidens came at a certain time. I lay lilies and roses. Silver is white and gold is red. The sun shines through the window. The bailiff carries off the bell. Nothing could be simpler and nothing could be much more obvious: indeed the statement about gold and silver is almost too obvious to merit stating. But when these several statements are put together into a combination of statements the simplicity vanishes. There is no apparent relationship whatever between the maidens' coming and the bailiff's going or between either of those events and the shining of the sun through the glass or the laying out of the robes in their folds. No amount of logical analysis, if you take these statements out of the poem and worry them there, will give you a meaning. And yet you feel — sense — the presence of meaning. Something is happening, is about to happen, which has significance upon it — something that involves all these unidentified players, the bailiff, the maidens, the lilies, the roses, the silver, the gold, the folded robes, the sun in the glass window, and "me" there in the middle of it. But what is it that is happening?

Perhaps, if we leave these unexplaining statements where they are, not attempting to worry their meaning out of them but letting their several meanings go over us like touch after touch of a light wind, the relationships will reveal themselves. "The maidens came / When I was in my mother's bower. / I had all that I wolde." That is, the maidens, whoever they

were, came, for whatever was to happen, while I was still
young, still in my mother's bower, still kept at home — while
I still had everything I wanted: words only a child still in
childhood would say. "The baily berith the bell away. . . ."
So there is ceremony of some kind to come: the bailiff and his
bell. "The lilly, the rose, the rose I lay. / The silver is whit,
red is the golde; / The robes they lay in fold. . . ." So I am
part of the preparation — I who lay out the lily and the rose,
as well as the maidens who fold the robes.

> *And through the glasse window shines the sone.*
> *How should I love and I so young?*

And suddenly these mysterious, elliptical relationships come
clear. We know now what the ceremony is. The sun shines
through the glass window of this house where I have had
everything I wanted, where I am still a child, and the
question illuminates everything — the young girl's question
— the question asked between lily and rose, between white
and red — "How should I love and I so young?"

What then can we say of the structure of the meanings
here? First, that it is illogical from the logical point of view
of expository prose. Second, that it is in every way different
from the orderly repetitions of the structure of sounds com-
posed by these same words. Third, that it only becomes
legible with that question "How should I love and I so
young" — that question the poignance of which we feel
though we should find it hard to explain our feeling in logical
or even reasonable terms. Finally, that it is a structure held
together not only, like the compositions of prose, by its own
skeleton of syntax, but by that other structure of sounds
with which it has so little apparent kinship. Try to read
it without the repetition of those refrains — "The baily

berith the bell away; / The lilly, the rose, the rose I lay" —
and see whether the question asked by the sun through the
glass is still a question the emotions comprehend.

But would conclusions of this kind be reached in the reading
of a more sophisticated and perfected poem? This ancient,
anonymous lyric is evidently a kind of folk song with the
folk song's weatherworn senselessness in sense. What of one
of the great poems of the literature, Shakespeare's Sonnet
CXVI?

> Let me not to the marriage of true minds
> Admit impediments. Love is not love
> Which alters when it alteration finds,
> Or bends with the remover to remove.
> O, no! it is an ever-fixèd mark,
> That looks on tempests and is never shaken;
> It is the star to every wand'ring bark,
> Whose worth's unknown, although his height be taken.
> Love's not Time's fool, though rosy lips and cheeks
> Within his bending sickle's compass come;
> Love alters not with his brief hours and weeks,
> But bears it out even to the edge of doom.
> If this be error and upon me proved,
> I never writ, nor no man ever loved.

Here again, if you look *through* the straightforward, logi-
cal structure of the English sonnet with its regular beat and
regular rhyme scheme, to the structure of meanings which
these same words compose, you will find a series of state-
ments. But here the statements, unlike the statements in
"The maidens came . . .," seem to be related to each other
in being related to the same subject. Each is a statement
about love. Each agrees with, or reinforces, the statements
which lie beside it. The effect of the whole is thus cumu-

lative and one could easily conclude that the structure of meanings is as logical and reasonable as the structure of the sounds. Indeed, there is only one difficulty in the way of that conclusion — the difficulty that none of these statements is in itself either reasonable or logical or even, if you will permit so inexact a word, true.

Remove them from the sonnet and set them out in sequence. There are, first of all, three general propositions stated flatly and without reservation: Love does not change even when the beloved changes; love does not alter with time; if these statements are not true no man ever loved and I never wrote — i.e., this sonnet was never written. Secondly, there is a series of assertions, mixed in with these general propositions, which state what love is: a navigation mark which no tempest can even shake; the North Star by which ships steer. Finally, there is a similar assertion about time: time has a sickle which lops rosy lips and cheeks.

None of us, faced with assertions like these in an ordinary prose composition, would find them very meaningful. Time has no sickle. Love is not a lighthouse. And as for the changelessness, the eternity, of love, we see little reason in the world around us, or in the fictions which re-create that world, to believe in either. Ours is a sensible scientific time and we know only too well where love, as Yeats puts it, has built its mansion. We have learned much about marriages through taking so many carefully apart. Virginity, if we may believe the novelists who seem to know most about these matters, is regarded in enlightened societies as something of an embarrassment. And every other American man and woman, if the statistics of the sociologists are well and truly collected, has learned about love, or tried to, in more ways than one.

But put these improbable statements back into the poem

where they exist and what happens? They *become* true. At least they become true for most readers of this sonnet — for right readers of it, to borrow Frost's word again. The marriage of true minds and the love which that marriage makes possible is a matter of faith for many who, whatever they may think, and however they may act in the world outside the poem, "know" in the poem's world that this marriage is possible and that this love does exist — exist forever.

How then does this sea-change come about? Because, as one of my students put it, this is not a poem about love, it is a poem about love as love is to a lover? Perhaps, but how is it then that love is true and is eternal not only to the lover truly in love who is imagined as speaking in the poem but to the reader centuries after who may not be in love at all? The answer to that question would seem to be the same as the answer to the question of meaning in "The maidens came . . .": the truth of Shakespeare's sonnet is a "felt" truth. It is not because we imagine a lover speaking what is true for *him* that we accept this truth. It is not, in other words, a merely dramatic experience that persuades us, like the experience of hearing Judith Anderson in *Medea*. It is a more personal and more immediate emotion than the shared emotion of the theater. We are *ourselves* this speaker in the poem and we know as he knows "in the heart" that in human life love *is* eternal sometimes: not only seems so — is. It is a paradox, of course. The knowledge which the emotions know is almost always paradoxical. Indeed it is for this reason that the sonnet ends with the poignant irony of those last two lines:

If this be error and upon me proved,
I never writ, nor no man ever loved.

Shakespeare knows as well as we that "this" *is* error. But we know too as well as Shakespeare that if this error could be "proved" then no one of us ever loved or ever will — nor has ever written of love either.

So that one concludes, I think, from a reading of this famous sonnet, that the structure of meanings in poetry may be not only a structure of disorder which emotion brings to order but a structure of untruth which emotion brings to truth.

Herrick's famous lyric "To Daffodils" adds another possibility:

> *Fair Daffodils, we weep to see*
> *You haste away so soon:*
> *As yet the early-rising Sun*
> *Has not attain'd his noon.*
> *Stay, stay*
> *Until the hasting day*
> *Has run*
> *But to the even-song;*
> *And, having pray'd together, we*
> *Will go with you along.*
>
> *We have short time to stay, as you,*
> *We have as short a Spring;*
> *As quick a growth to meet decay*
> *As you, or any thing.*
> *We die,*
> *As your hours do, and dry*
> *Away,*
> *Like to the Summer's rain;*
> *Or as the pearls of morning's dew*
> *Ne'er to be found again.*

Here, the problem is not one of complication of meaning but of apparent emptiness of meaning. If you take the sayings of the poem out of the poem you have little more than the obvious banality of the observation that life is brief — that men are as mortal as daffodils. If however you put the sayings back into the poem something seems to happen to this banality. I can best describe the change for myself by saying that these statements cease to be *obviously* true and become, instead, *meaningfully* true. We all of us know, or think we know, that we are mortal, that our days are as grass, that we are here today and gone tomorrow. But in Herrick's poem we *are* mortal — all at once and without warning we *become* this knowledge we think we possess and we are shaken by it.

> *Stay, stay*
> *Until the hasting day*
> *Has run*
> *But to the even-song;*
> *And, having pray'd together, we*
> *Will go with you along.*

I have a favorite parable which expresses this sea-change for me. It is by Ivor Richards out of Robert Oppenheimer out of Professor Dirac — a three story mountain — and it goes as follows. Professor Dirac walked one day into his laboratory in Berlin or wherever and spotted young Oppenheimer, recently graduated from Harvard, among the apprentices. "Ah," said he (Oppenheimer reporting), "I understand you combine the writing of poetry with the study of physics." Oppenheimer pleaded guilty. "I simply don't understand it," sighed the great man. "In science you try to say what nobody has known before in such a way that everybody will understand it, whereas in *poetry* . . ." And he stalked out to a chorus of applauding laughter. But when Ivor Richards heard the tale he turned its author's triumph inside out with a single word: "Precisely!" And of course he was right. In poetry you *do* try to say what everybody has "known before" in such a way that nobody will "understand" it, and when you succed you say something at least as significant as that famous Second Law of Thermodynamics which C. P. Snow has now established as the basic test of the new literacy. Herrick does it here. He says what everybody thinks he "knows" — that life is brief — that we all die — but says it in such a way that nobody can merely "understand" it and thus file it in the memory to be forgotten. In the poem he must *feel* it, *face* it, *live* it. Nobody "understands" this conversation between men and flowers or, indeed, this world in which flowers "haste away" and men and flowers pray together. And the result is that nobody can deal with this conversation as we all of us deal with our easy "understandings" of life and death and the world we live in. On the contrary everybody — everybody, that is, who truly reads this poem — is compelled, for the moment at least, to face the reality of his knowledge and to live his death:

> *And, having pray'd together, we*
> *Will go with you along.*

Here, then, the structure of the words as signs is a structure which, within the other structure of sounds, turns apparent meaninglessness to meaning and accomplishes it in the same way as the metamorphosis was accomplished in Shakespeare's sonnet and in "The maidens came . . .": by an enhancement of emotion.

But this word, emotion, is itself subject to misinterpretation and nowhere more than in the university where reason is

the proprietor in residence and every other comer is accused
of trespass. It is on this account that I should like to refer
this discussion to the third section of Pound's "Hugh Selwyn
Mauberley."

The tea-rose tea-gown, etc.
Supplants the mousseline of Cos,
The pianola "replaces"
Sappho's barbitos.

Christ follows Dionysus,
Phallic and ambrosial
Made way for macerations;
Caliban casts out Ariel.

All things are a flowing,
Sage Heracleitus says;
But a tawdry cheapness
Shall outlast our days.

Even the Christian beauty
Defects — after Samothrace;
We see τὸ καλὸν
Decreed in the market place.

Faun's flesh is not to us,
Nor the saint's vision.
We have the press for wafer;
Franchise for circumcision.

All men, in law, are equals.
Free of Pisistratus,
We choose a knave or an eunuch
To rule over us.

O bright Apollo,
τίν' ἀνδρα, τίν' ἤρωα, τίνα θεὸν,
What god, man, or hero,
Shall I place a tin wreath upon!

Here the organization of the words as meanings is "modern" in "the most modern way." Pound's use of "explicit rendering," meaning the presentation of the subject not by a generalizing description but by a specific figure, or name, or quotation, or fragment of quotation, standing *for* the subject has become standard "modern" practice. The theory is — and it is a fairly persuasive theory — that the true poetic act consists in the presentation of the reality of experience directly in its own often irrelevant terms leaving the reader to puzzle out the pattern of relationships for himself as he is left to puzzle it out in life, rather than having the particulars strained through a sieve of generalizations and presented to him as a series of progressive steps in a logical argument prepared in advance. He will see more *seeingly*, the theory goes, if he is exposed, in all the nakedness of a perhaps temporary bewilderment, to selected moments of human experience which may at first have no pattern but which, in the end, will add up.

The making out of the meaning, therefore, involves processes which even intellectuals can accept as intellectual. Here, for example, you have such particulars as the Greek island of Cos and its exquisite mousselines which revealed the loveliness of a woman's body moving under. You have Sappho's lyre by a more recondite name. You have phallic and ambrosial Dionysus with all that that little constellation of words implies to the classicist. You have Christ of the macerations. You have old Heraclitus with his philosophy of flow. You have *tó kalón*, faun's flesh, the eucharistic wafer, the benevolent tyrant Pisistratus and a slightly garbled quotation from Pindar's "Second Olympian Ode." Enough, added up together, to keep a graduate student explicating through a dozen pages of a Ph.D. thesis. But when he got through what would he have? A notion as banal in its explicated form as the theme of Herrick's "Daffodils": the good old times are gone. If there is a staler or more boring idea in the whole herring barrel of human cogitation I don't know what it is. There has probably never been a time, from the beginning of times, when living men did not regret the past — or what they took for the past. If our first forefather ever turns up as we excavate for our last shelter, his eye sockets will be turned backward toward the happy creeping fish who lived a life of harmony and restraint in the slime of the evaporating marshes. But suppose you de-explicate these scholarly particulars and put the whole paraphernalia back into the poem. What happens then? The banality disappears. The loss becomes real. The regret becomes tragic. And why? Because a passion of indignation transforms it. The power of true poetry which conquered the vacuity of innocence in Herrick's "Daffodils" conquers the vacuity of academicism here and the empty meaning *means*.

Four poems do not provide a body of proof sufficient to support a general proposition, but when they are poems as different as these, and when they share, as these do, common characteristics, a tentative conclusion may seem justified. In all four the structure of meanings is different from the structure of meanings in prose. It lacks logical order or logical relevance or logical truth or logical content. It cannot be removed from the structure of sound without crumbling away like a Peruvian mummy: removed from the poem it no longer means. But *in* the poem this illogical meaning *comes* to mean — and comes to mean in all four poems in the same way — by the touch of feeling. By the sun through the glass window. By men and flowers bowed together. By the quiet irony of the voice that says: "If this be error and upon me proved, / I never writ, nor no man ever loved." By the angry bitterness of the very different voice which cries: "We have the press for wafer; / Franchise for circumcision." It is when the illogical meanings are tried, as Keats said, *on the pulses* that the illogic disappears. The structure of meanings which the reason cannot find — or can find only to destroy — exists in the emotions. It is meaning carried, as Wordsworth put it, alive into the heart with passion.

But if this is true of the structure of the words as meanings then what conclusion can be reached as to the structure of the poem as a whole — the poem as a whole which is composed of words which in their meanings are what we see and in their sounds so different — so orderly — so logical — so much more orderly and logical than the structure of words ever is outside of poetry? There Coleridge must speak for us — or at least for me. What is poetry, Coleridge asks himself in the *Biographia Literaria*. "This question," he replies, "is nearly the same as the question, what is a poet?" And he goes on to his famous definition: The poet "brings the whole soul of man into activity. He diffuses a tone and spirit that blends and, as it were, fuses [the faculties] each into each by that synthetic and magical power to which I would exclusively appropriate the name of imagination. This power reveals itself in the balance or reconcilement of discordant qualities . . . a more than usual state of emotion with more than usual order."

CHAPTER THREE

Images

IT IS in that balance, that reconcilement, that the double structure of poetry composes itself. The "synthetic and magical power" which "brings the whole soul of man into activity" — "that synthetic and magical power to which I would exclusively appropriate the name of imagination" — is a power which poets possess only in and through their poems. And the "balance or reconcilement of discordant qualities" through which this power reveals itself must therefore be a balance or reconcilement in the poem itself.

But if the reconcilement exists in the poem then the things reconciled must exist there also — the "more than usual state of emotion" and the "more than usual order." And it is this suggestion that tempts the pursuer of poetry out to the crumbling edge of caution. If the order and the emotion are there in the poem awaiting reconcilement *where* are they in the poem and how did they get there?

One can guess at the "more than usual order." It seems to be staring back at you out of the printed page when you look at a poem. In no other use of words, not even their use in the formal documents of the law, is order as obvious as it is in a poem. Everything is verbally ordered — and in what used to be called "free verse" quite as much as in regular verse. The writer of a poem is not a cow hand trying to throw a steer with a rope which can run loose and respond to every pull and drag. He is much more like those net fishermen you see in the Pacific Islands and along the Spanish shore who take their catch by throwing their nets in such a way that they take shape — lovely shape — in the air and fall in pattern. Old Lu Chi's metaphor of the trapper of Heaven and Earth in the cage of form says it all: the cage *is* form — palpable form — order — an order which would be "unusual" anywhere.

But what of the "more than usual state of emotion"? Where in the poem does the more than usual state of emotion reside as the more than usual order resides in the verbal pattern of the words as sounds? Can it be flushed, perhaps, in the same thicket? Is it the pattern of sounds that evokes, also, the heightened emotion? Certainly sounds can move us — even sounds divorced from sense — and not only the lovely sounds of music either. Mere beat and bang appear to affect the modern adolescent as pipes in India affect the snake. And the phenomenon is not limited to adolescents. Vachel Lindsay who is not much read now — though he will be again — experimented with poetic beat and bang some forty years ago with startling consequences:

> *Walk with care, walk with care,*
> *Or Mumbo-Jumbo, God of the Congo,*
> *And all of the other*
> *Gods of the Congo,*
> *Mumbo Jumbo will hoodoo you.*

Beware, beware, walk with care,
Boomlay, boomlay, boomlay, boom.
Boomlay, boomlay, boomlay, boom,
Boomlay, boomlay, boomlay, boom,
Boomlay, boomlay, boomlay,
BOOM

That poems like "The Congo" could excite audiences when Lindsay read them is, of course, an inadequate statement. He read his "Daniel" to a Bloomsbury audience in 1920 and all literary London joined in the refrain:

King Darius said to the lions: —
"Bite Daniel. Bite Daniel.
Bite him. Bite him. Bite him!"

and the crowd, according to Lindsay's biographer, Eleanor Ruggles, "joined in, rocking, stamping and roaring at the word of command":

THUS roared the lions:
"We want Daniel, Daniel, Daniel,
We want Daniel, Daniel, Daniel!
Grrrrrrrrrrrrrrrrrrrrrrrrrrr
Grrrrrrrrrrrrrrrrrrrrrrrrrrrrr"

And it wasn't only the Woolfs, the Stracheys, and the Sitwells either. When Robert Graves brought Lindsay to Oxford more or less as a practical joke and arranged an evening recital with Sir Walter Raleigh, Professor of English Literature, in the chair, the dons solemnly spaced in the front rows and the undergraduates, about a thousand of them, lined up behind in gowns and mortarboards, some rather un-English consequences followed. "By two minutes," says Graves, "he had the respectable and intellectual and cynical audience listening. By ten, intensely excited; by twenty, elated and losing self-control . . . by forty minutes roaring like a bonfire . . ."

This would have to be described, I should say, as a more than usual state of emotion, and some of it, at least, was aroused by words used for almost purely percussive purposes. But I doubt that Coleridge would have regarded the scene as an illustration of his theory. The emotions he had in mind were emotions which the sounds of words might affect but hardly in so direct a way. Something more than rhythms, however exciting, would have to be in play if "the whole soul of man" were to respond. Where then, in a poem-itself, is the source and spring of this unusual state of emotion to be found? If it is not solely the work of the rhythms and the beat, what is it the work of? The answer would seem to have to be: of the meanings. The structure of the meanings is in some way involved. But how is it involved? Directly by issuing commands to the emotions to excite themselves? By directing the whole soul of man to feel love or to feel loss or whatever? There is a song on the radio these mornings along about shaving time which informs the allegedly listening audience that:

Myyyyyy Heaaaaaart Criiiiiies for you
Myyyyyy Heaaaaaart Sighs for you
Myyyyyy Heaaaaaart Dies for you.

This information interferes in no way with the movement of my razor.

But if the bald announcement of emotion does not suffice, how then *is* emotion contained in a poem — emotion, that is, over and above the emotion excited by the beat and sound

of the lines? I suppose I should be well advised not to ask —
or not, at least, to ask in cold print — or, in any event, not to
ask in public and then attempt an answer. These are dark and
difficult questions which involve speculations no practicer of
the art of poetry is in a position to pursue: they require new
philosophical examinations — revolutionary aesthetic theories
— scientific experiments by the masters of new sciences. But
the fact is, unfortunately, that I have no choice. Once com-
mitted to the pursuit of the unicorn you must follow where
the trail leads — and the trail leads precisely to this precipice.
If the sense of a poem is a sense tried upon the pulses rather
than a sense spelled out by the reason, then there is no escape
from the question which asks: What set the pulses beating so?
One asks it because one must. But one would be well advised
to answer it in the spirit of our ancient friend Lu Chi, who,
you will remember, concluded the introduction to his Wen
Fu, his Fu on letters, with the sentence: "Nevertheless, what I
am able to say I have put down here." Whereupon he crooned
the clean fragrance of past worthies, rinsed his mouth with the
extract of the Six Arts, and began.

I should like to begin in the same way — with humility and
the clean fragrance of a worthy, dead two thousand years
— together with the comment of a former student of mine.
The dead worthy is the Emperor Wu-ti who ruled in the
Celestial Kingdom until 87 B.C. and who is remembered for a
poem about his mistress, "Li Fu-jen." This is Arthur Waley's
translation:

> The sound of her silk skirt has stopped.
> On the marble pavement dust grows.
> Her empty room is cold and still.
> Fallen leaves are piled against the doors.
> Longing for that lovely lady
> How can I bring my aching heart to rest?

My student's comment related to the poem's end. "This," she said, "is a mere statement. It shouldn't make me feel anything. But in its place in the poem it does. Can it be," she asked, "that these four images placed there side by side somehow enhance the flat statement which follows them? If the emperor had merely said that his heart ached there would have been no poem. But there is." And she went on to talk about those images — how they touch the three senses and perhaps a fourth if that heap of fallen leaves smells as dead leaves do —

> *The sound of her silk skirt has stopped.*
> *On the marble pavement dust grows.*
> *Her empty room is cold and still.*
> *Fallen leaves are piled against the doors.*

— how they are all images of absence: that sound of the silk skirt is a sound which is not there; that dust "growing" (wonderful verb) on the marble pavement is dust which says that no feet walk there any more; that cold room is a room once warm; those fallen leaves against the sill are leaves from another year. And all this is, of course, true. These images are mirror images, images backwards, images the eye accepts too easily and something else must therefore understand. They draw emotion in as air is drawn into a vacuum and when, at the end, the emperor speaks for himself in words which, standing alone, would have had no power over us, the emotion understands and gathers meaning round them.

> *Longing for that lovely lady*
> *How can I bring my aching heart to rest?*

As another student pointed out, that word "rest" takes on an extraordinary poignance in the shadow of those four images. Everything in the poem has come to rest — the sound of silk, the feet on the floor, the warmth of the room, the leaves — everything but his heart.

The implications of all this are hopeful. Whatever science and philosophy may conclude about the mysterious relationship between art and emotion and the power of the one over the other, there would seem to be, nevertheless, a small acre here in which the rest of us may walk around with a modest confidence that something interesting can perhaps be observed. Images in a poem do seem to have some relationship to the emotion a poem contains, and an examination of the way images work would thus appear to promise at least a hint of light. I propose, therefore, to attempt such an examination here. But I propose to attempt it in a way which requires some justification in advance, for the poems I wish to use are poems in a language few of us, and certainly not I myself, can read. They are poems, furthermore, the latest of which was written more than a thousand years ago. And they come from a country on the other side of the world which no American can now visit and which few were ever able truly to understand.

Why turn to Chinese poems from the *Book of Odes* and from the great age of T'ang for an examination of the way images work in poetry? For two reasons. Let me begin with the larger. Poetry is poetry in all tongues. Language differences do, of course, produce differences in form and particularly in prosody, but a poem in one language is comparable with a poem in another for both are poems. There is more true difference, or was, between Japanese music and European music than between a Japanese seventeen-syllable *hokku* and an epitaph from the Greek Anthology or an English epigram by, say, Landor. The *Encyclopeadia Britan-*

nica demonstrates that proposition when, having opined that Japanese poetry is "without known counterpart" elsewhere in the world, it goes on to quote, by way of illustration, the well-known hokku which translates: "More fleeting than the glint of withered leaf on the wind, the thing called life."

The second, and smaller, but more relevant reason is that images and their relation to each other and to a given poem are more *visible* in Chinese poetry than in English or in any European literature. Ordinarily, in English, statements — including, particularly, statements which present images — are linked together by some grammatical device — some external indication of the nature of the relationship intended: "as if," "as though," "like," "Like two proud armies marching in the field," "Shall I compare thee to a summer's day." But in a line of Chinese poetry there are no grammatical devices to indicate the relations of words to each other. There is no inflection, no agglutination. The relationship is left to be inferred from the context, from the logic of the situation. The characters, each of them representing a root idea, stand there side by side with their graphic backgrounds, like imaginary shadows, off behind them. The sounds follow each other reticently in their sequence. And the verbal meaning is divined, not, as in English, by solving the syntax, but by letting these root ideas take their places in a pattern they compose together.

How this character of the language affects the presentation and relationship of images, a line of Chinese poetry translated literally for me by Professor J. R. Hightower will demonstrate. It is a line from a poem by the great Tu Fu, greatest of T'ang poets and one of the gigantic figures of the poetry of our human world. The poem as a whole goes thus, in an English rendering made under the editorship of Robert Payne:

The good rain knows when to fall,
Coming in this spring to help the seeds,
Choosing to fall by night with a friendly wind,
Silently moistening the whole earth.
Over this silent wilderness the clouds are dark.
The only light shines from a river boat.
Tomorrow morning everything will be red and wet
And all Chengtu will be covered with blossoming flowers.

It is the sixth line I asked Professor Hightower to translate: "The only light shines from a river boat." In English — at least in the English of Payne's translation — this line conveys nothing sharply visible or sensible. One registers the fact that the rainy night is dark except for a light of some unspecified kind on a boat out in the river. But in literal translation the five characters of the line are freed to stand by themselves and for themselves:

RIVER . . . BOAT . . . FIRE . . . ALONE . . . BRIGHT

And at once and inescapably one begins to *see*. Under those dark clouds in this black and silent wilderness there is a river, and on the river a boat and on the boat fire — such a cook fire probably as you see on the decks of river craft and small fishing vessels throughout the East. Moreover, besides this spark out there on the river there is nothing else that shines, nothing else bright. This fire is alone. The omission of connectives, enclitics, tools of syntax, directives for understanding — the absence of all this, though it makes the deciphering of the line difficult for the reasoning faculties, arouses the sensual imagination and one sees, one hears, one almost catches the scent of that rain-wet earth which will be red and white — that earth of Chengtu which, tomorrow morning, will be covered with flowers.

But it is not only images *as* images a Chinese poem can make you see. Here is another literally translated line of Tu Fu's from a poem about that unending civil war which ravaged the China of the T'ang in the eighth century and ravaged the greater part of Tu Fu's life with it:

BLUE ... SMOKE ... BEACON-FIRES ... WHITE ... BONES ... MEN

The grammatical connectives supply themselves: "The blue is the smoke of beacon-fires: the white is bones." But something else supplies itself as you look at that blue smoke and those white bones. The blue of smoke is *now*. Smoke is always now. It is only as the smoke blows now that we see it blue or white or grey or black on the air. But these bones of men are not now. They are long ago. They are white. So that these two images are seen with time between them. Blue is the smoke of war — of this war — of this war now up here in the northwest where these bail fires, these watch fires, never go out, their acrid wood smoke blowing blue on the thin cold air. White are the bones of men — of men killed long ago — of men killed long ago in this endless war that never ends. *Time* haunts these images set there side by side: time haunted by war and war haunted by time. And it is the two images that hold that tragedy of time and war between them.

It is because Chinese poetry, in the hands of its masters, uses its images in this laconic and explicit way that I wish to press my question among Chinese masterpieces rather than in the poetry of our own tongue where we are blinded by familiarity and grammar. But these great poems cannot and should not be used in translation as mere examples. They exist, and vividly exist, in their own right and ideally they should be seen whole — heard whole — before they are called to witness. For, as it happens, Chinese poetry has as complicated an ordering of sound as the poetry of any literature. The line (I follow Professor Hightower's description) is the unit of construction in Chinese prosody, because the Chinese language is — or was in classical times — monosyllabic, and the multisyllabic words which provide accented and unaccented sounds within the word, long and short quantities, in English and French and Greek and Latin, were therefore nonexistent. Rhythms within the line being unavailable, the line itself was made to serve as rhythmic unit: a four-word, which is to say a four-sound, line was employed down to early Han times, two centuries or so before our era, when a five-word line was introduced, and thereafter a line of seven words was added. But the beat was not as simple as this description suggests, for the five-word line observed a pause or sense of pause — a caesura — after the second word, and the seven-word line observed a caesura after the fourth word so that the five-word beat was syncopated against 2:3 and the seven against 4:3.

Nor was this all. Chinese, because of its monosyllabic character, is rich — or poor — in homophones, words which sound alike but mean differently, as bear, bare and bear in English: to carry, to be naked or to be covered with fur. Professor Hightower tells me that modern Mandarin Chinese has at its disposal only about four hundred syllable sounds to enunciate a vocabulary as rich as ours. The result is — or was, millennia ago — that means of differentiation had to be found. In written Chinese the means were found in the proliferation of the characters which signify the words, a special character for each word and thus an "alphabet," if I may be excused the term, of thousands of characters. But in spoken Chinese this device would not serve and a solution was found elsewhere — in what is called *tone*. By changing the pitch of the many-meaninged sound, or the direction of the change of pitch, your nakedness is turned to an animal or sent off to produce a child.

I speak of this as a solution. Of course it was nothing of the kind. It came into being with the words and as part of the words. But it was not until the fifth century of our era that the poets of the Celestial Kingdom took professional cognizance of it. Poets are always wading and seining at the edge of the slow flux of language for something they can fish out and put to their own uses, and the various tones, four in number around Peking and eight or nine around Canton (had those cities then existed) were precisely such a find. The result was "regulated verse" in which the position of the tones in the line and in a sequence of lines is predetermined. You thus have, by the time you get to the two great poets of the T'ang Dynasty, tone patterns imposed upon caesura patterns imposed on patterns of line length. To speak of the resultant structure as exhibiting "more than usual order" would seem to me permissible.

With this necessary digression to remind ourselves how much of these poems we are *not* talking about when we talk of them here, let me return to the T'ang poets and specifically to Li Po and his poem on waking from drunkenness. A rough paraphrase aimed primarily at the relation of the images might go like this:

"Life in the world is nothing but a big dream:
I won't spoil it by doing anything or troubling about anything,"
I said. So I was drunk all day—
Lay out on the porch in front of the door helpless.
When I woke I stared at the garden—
Some bird was singing in the flowers.
I wondered: what season is it?
Chattering oriole: spring wind.
Moved by that singing I sighed.

There was wine so I filled my cup.
I sang madly waiting for the moon.
When the song ended sense had gone.

This is not only a famous poem: it is also a useful one, and one particularly useful to us in our examination of the possible relation between images and emotion. Readers of poems in English-speaking countries suffer from a predisposition, common as the common cold, to assume that images in poems are decorations and should, therefore, be "beautiful." There is even a tendency among some of the more inveterate sufferers to describe a really ravishing image as "poetic." If they are right it is obvious that Li Po was wrong. Getting drunk may be "poetic" to enthusiastic souls but there is nothing "poetic" about coming undrunk and even less about falling back into drunkenness for a second time in a single day. Furthermore it is fairly obvious that Li Po was as conscious of that fact as we are. No one who reads this poem more than once can believe it is written in celebration of drunkenness. The spring wind and the singing bird alone would make that clear. No, these images are not decorations and were not meant to be — are not beautiful and were not meant to be. They are elements of the poem, elements of its structure, and if they are to be read they must be read in this sense.

I suppose I ought not to labor the point though I should dearly like to. I know of no greater obstacle to the successful reading of poems than precisely this presupposition that poems are "beautiful" and that their images are "beautiful" and that the more "beautiful" their images, and the *more* "beautiful" images they exhibit — the more pearls on the string — the better poems they are. Poems are not meant to be beautiful: they are meant to be poems — which is something at once more and less. Images in poems are not meant to be beautiful: they are meant to be images in poems, working as images in poems work. And no one knew all this better than Li Po and his countrymen who had had a longer experience of poetry than any other nation and whose skill precisely as makers of images has never been equalled, either in paint or ink or words. The highest praise the old critics could give the poet T'ao Yuan-Ming was to say: "His emotions are real, his scenery is real, his facts are real and his thoughts are real." In what sense real? Drawn from the life. It was T'ao Yuan-Ming who wrote the famous lines: "Winds from warmer climates ruffle the early dawn: whoever comes must go . . ."

Well, Li Po's facts are real — too real for some tastes — and Li Po's scenery is real: his drunken man waking, blinking at the garden lawn, hearing the single bird, the spring wind. But are they merely real — these little scenes? Do they compose, as one of my students put it, nothing more than the "reminiscences of an Oriental inebriate"? Or do they contain something more or other than themselves? Why are they not merely idle or irrelevant or meaningless?

For a reason which they themselves reveal and which no reflective reader will ignore. These images exist in a *relationship*. There are two drunkennesses here and they are not the same. The first, as one of my students put it, is passive: the second is active. The first is a drunkenness fallen into on a spring morning in the mood of that little saying at the start of the poem — a mood we all know — Life is a big dream: I won't spoil it by doing anything. The second is a passionate drunkenness; a drunkenness wildly singing, waiting for the moon to rise; a drunkenness which ends in a kind of death — sense gone. There they stand at the beginning and end of the poem — those two drunken men who are the same man. And between them — what? Between them a garden and a singing bird and the spring wind — these three and a question: "I wondered: what season is it?" And what does that question mean? It means that I do not know where I am in time. And what have the bird and the wind to do with that realization? *They* know and *I* do not: "Chattering oriole: spring wind." The wind knew what the season was and the bird knew but I did not know. Time had gone by me. Life had gone by me. I had lost a moment out of time, a moment out of life. I fill my cup again. Wildly singing I wait for the moon to rise . . . that *moment*.

What lies between these two drunken men in this garden in the spring in other words is a recognition, an awareness, an awareness of the mortal condition, a glimpse of man in that net of time in which we are all caught and whose tangling threads we cherish. Life in the world is a big dream — yes, on a spring morning in the sun: something not to be spoiled by taking thought. But to wake and find a day of that dream gone — not even to know the time or season of the year — though the wind knows and the bird knows . . . life is no longer a big dream then. Life in its loss, even in the loss of a day, of a part of a day, of a few hours, is dear. Passionately dear. Beyond price.

I suppose it would be possible — indeed, I know it would be possible — to read this poem without emotion of any kind. Anyone who learns the apparently historical fact that Li Po was himself a famous consumer of rice wine, and who knows the familiar literary fact that the celebration of drunkenness was a standard theme of Chinese poetry, might very well conclude that these particular verses compose nothing more than a vulgar and rather stupid literary pleasantry. Certainly there is nothing in the language of the poem to suggest that the emotions are supposed to be involved. The language has no explicit design upon our feelings. We are not being told to grieve or smile. There is no visible intention to wring the heart or even to touch it. But nevertheless and notwithstanding there is feeling here for any man who will read not merely the language of the poem but the images in eye and ear which the language presents. It is when we *see* these two drunken men who are the same man, and when we *hear* the bird and the wind that that question becomes a question we understand.

The emotion, if there is emotion, is in the images — or, if not in them, then among them. As it so often is in Chinese poems. There is another poem of Li Po's, a poem of leave-taking, which begins, in Pound's translation: "Light rain is on the light dust." One wonders why those simple words go so unerringly home. Because the smell of dust in the first few drops of rain, the light rain, is a sad smell? Or is it for another reason? Is it because, to see the light rain on the light dust one must stand, head bowed, looking down at the earth at one's feet? Whichever it is, this grief is a grief known first, as grief in the world so often is, in the senses — the senses as these images have touched them.

But it is not always in this direct and almost physical way that Li Po's images work. There is a poem he calls ironically a "Song of War." Robert Payne's translation goes like this:

> *Before the Peak of Returning Joy the sand was like snow.*
> *Outside the surrendered city the moon was like frost.*
> *I do not know who blew the horns at night,*
> *But all night long the boys looked toward their homes.*

These are statements, you see: laconic statements which suggest images, or are images. There is a peak called the Peak of Returning Joy — a peak, apparently, which one would see joyfully from the frontier returning home. There is a city which has been surrendered. There is a desert before that peak where the sand is *like* snow. Outside the city the moon is *like* frost . . . (so it is not yet winter but one thinks of winter). There are horns blown at night: I do not know who blew them. There is an army and boys in it who, all night long, look toward their homes. Hope of returning? Despair of returning? In a long war, as our generation has learned to know, this hope and this despair are the same. But whatever it is, despair or hope, the despair, the hope, is *in* these images, *among* them. Is it less poignant for that or is it more poignant? Is it less well said because there is no explicit word of emotion? — nothing to tell us how to feel, despair *or* hope? — or is it better said?

The beginning of Pound's translation of Li Po's "Bridge at Ten Shin" (Pound calls Li Po "Rihaku" because he came to him through Fenellosa who worked in Japan) makes the point:

> *March has come to the bridge head,*
> *Peach boughs and apricot boughs hang over a thousand gates,*
> *At morning there are flowers to cut the heart,*
> *And evening drives them on the eastward-flowing waters.*
> *Petals are on the gone waters and on the going,*
>   *And on the back-swirling eddies,*
> *But to-day's men are not the men of the old days,*
> *Though they hang in the same way over the bridge-rail. . . .*

Men leaning over a bridge. Petals "on the gone water and on the going." And among them? Time and change. Change and time. The sea is the same color at dawn and the moon still goes down over the gates in the same way and the princes still stand in rows and the lords ride out to the borders and go proudly in to the banquets and the food and the perfumed air and the dancing girls and the flutes — everything is the same and they think it will last forever. Other men have thought this too, haven't they? But it is one thing to think it idly between two other thoughts, brushing the shadow away with a shake of the head, and another thing altogether to think it between the petals on the gone water and the petals on the going.

This Li Po knew and Chinese poetry had known it before him for a long time — perhaps two thousand years before the eighth century of our era in which he lived. There is a poem in the *Book of Odes* collected in the fifth or sixth century B.C. — tradition says by Confucius — which shows how old the knowledge is.

> *Dead doe lies in forest,*
> *White rushes cover her.*
> *Lady thinking of the spring,*
> *Fine knight over her.*
>
> *In the oak forest,*
> *In the waste land, doe is laid:*
> *White rushes over her.*
> *Lady beautiful as jade.*
>
> *Don't please touch me, Sir.*
> *Don't snatch my handkerchief away . . .*
> *Don't! My dog will bark.*

There is a dead doe, slender body, on the forest floor covered with white rushes. There is a yearning lady covered by a fine knight. They are the same? The one mistaken for the other? No. The poem repeats itself. In the oakenshaw, in the waste land, there is a dead doe. White rushes are over *her*. There is a lady beautiful as jade. So there are two images, like but unlike. How unlike? As unlike as the stillness of the dead doe under her rushes and the laughing girl with her absurd remonstrance: "Don't! My dog will bark!" . . . (somebody might see us!). A No turned Yes in the words that say it.

Discussion of this poem can move in circles unless one realizes that this is not — or not merely — a narrative. These two like and unlike images lie side by side in time as well as place. Indeed, that is the whole point and meaning — that they lie side by side: the girl beautiful as jade at the moment of most intense life which balances so precariously on the edge of the ridiculous with its "Don't! Don't!"; and there beside it in the same scene, the same time, that other body slender as hers, soft as hers, but dead, not alive, and covered not with love but with white grasses. But what then is the emotion of the poem? Grief for the dead doe? Amusement at the giggling girl? Neither the one nor the other. The emotion is in the place between — the place where they are together — where they meet, as indeed they do meet in our lives though we have no words to say it: death and passion, the human comedy and indifferent death.

But can we draw conclusions from these poems — conclusions as to the power of imagery to contain emotion in poetry in general? Or are these poems examples of nothing but the use of images in the poetry of China? I think they are something more. I think so, first, because the art of poetry is, as I have said, essentially the same in all languages however surface appearances may differ. I think so, in the second place, because the same use of images will be found in our own language though concealed under grammatical devices and habits of familiarity. With us too you will find a statement and another statement beside it — quite a different statement — one that would seem to have little or no relation to the first. There is a man, in Marvell's "To His Coy Mistress," begging his girl to love him. There is behind him the sound of a hurrying chariot clattering across the plain. There is a man in love. There is a proud ship standing in toward shore. Ordinarily, as I said earlier, these side-by-side statements are tied together in English by grammatical rigging, words of

comparison, words of contrast. But not always. There are no
such stage directions in

> *The baily berith the bell away;*
> *The lilly, the rose, the rose I lay.*
>
> *The silver is whit, red is the golde;*
> *The robes they lay in fold.*

and neither are there such external aids in that loveliest of
all English songs:

> *O westron wind when wilt thou blow*
> *That the small rain down can rain?*
> *Christ that my love were in my arms*
> *And I in my bed again.*

Here the two little scenes of wind and weather and love and
bed are left side by side to mean if they can. And they do
mean. The poem is not a poem about the one or the other.
It is not a poem about weather. And neither is it a poem about
making love. The emotion it holds is held between these
two statements in the place where love and time cross each
other. Here, as in those old Chinese poems, the emotion,
somehow contained in the poem, is an emotion which words
cannot come at directly — which no words as words can
describe. *How* will you "describe" in words the poignancy of
the recognition of the *obstacle* of time — its recognition not
on the clock face or among the stars but on the nerves of
the body and in the blood itself? But if you cannot "describe"
it in words how then can words contain it? Well, how do they
contain it here? By *not* speaking of it. By *not* speaking of it
at all. By speaking of something else, something off at the
one side and the other as the man at the helm of a ship looks

off and above to starboard and larboard to see the channel marker before him in the dark. By speaking of two things which, like parentheses, can include between them what neither of them says. By leaving a space between one sensed image and another where what cannot be said can *be* — this sensuous, this bodily knowledge of the defeat of love by time — this When? When? Ah when? — When will the wind go west and the spring rain come to bring her back to me and me to her?

I think for myself, perhaps too confidently, that it is in some such way as this that emotion is contained by images in a poem — in some such way as this that the more than usual state of emotion, when images induce it, is brought about. No single image can create the degree of emotion Coleridge speaks of, but the juxtaposition of images or image-like statements can create it — and can create it even though — or perhaps because — the juxtaposition is inexplicable to the faculties of reason: men praying with flowers, a laughing girl and a dead doe, the mariners' star and the loyalty of love. There may be many images and image-like statements set down side by side as in Shakespeare's sonnet on the marriage of true minds, or there may be no more than two as in "O westron wind . . ." or "Dead doe . . ." and one of the two may, as in Frost's poem called "The Most of It" — the poem of the buck crossing the lake — be assumed or implied but when the emotion is in the images there is always a relationship between images — *not* an image in isolation. The philosophers tell us that anything we can know must exist in a relationship. Certainly it is true of anything we can feel. That ancient Greek fragment on the sinking moon, once attributed to Sappho, is a poem and not an archaeological curiosity precisely because it contains not only the Greek sky beyond the lintel of the door but an aging lonely woman lying staring at it in the night:

The moon is down and the Pleiades.
It is the middle of the night.
And time passes, time passes,
And I lie alone . . .

CHAPTER FOUR

Metaphor

I F THE Chinese poems we have examined are true poems —
and the test of time would indicate that they are — then we
may conclude, I think, that one of the means to meaning in
this art is a certain relationship of images: what might be
called a coupling of images, though the coupling may include
more images than two. One image is established by words
which make it sensuous and vivid to the eyes or ears or touch
— to any of the senses. Another image is put beside it. And
a meaning appears which is neither the meaning of one image
nor the meaning of the other nor even the sum of both but
a *consequence* of both — a consequence of both in their con-
junction, in their relation to each other. There is the blue
smoke of war. There are the white bones of men. And there
is the heaviness of time in the space between them.

Suppose we press the examination a little further. What is
the nature of this meaning which coupled images can contain?
Is it emotional only — sadness for that unending war, for all
the unending wars, for ourselves in our own time caught be-

tween the white bones of our brothers killed forty-two years ago in another country and that enormous mushroom of fiery poisoned smoke on the horizon now? Is that all those images contain? For some, perhaps. And for some, perhaps, it is enough. To feel emotion is at least to feel. The crime against life, the worst of all crimes, is *not* to feel. And there was never, perhaps, a civilization in which that crime, the crime of torpor, of lethargy, of apathy, the snake-like sin of coldness-at-the-heart, was commoner than in our technological civilization in which the emotionless emotions of adolescent boys are mass produced on television screens to do our feeling for us, and a woman's longing for her life is twisted, by singing commercials, into a longing for a new detergent, family size, which will keep her hands as innocent as though she had never lived. It is the modern painless death, this commercialized atrophy of the heart. None of us is safe from it. The intellectual life can become technological too no matter what its content, and Acedy, you may recall, was the occupational sin of the medieval clerks. If poetry can call our numbed emotions to life, its plain human usefulness needs no further demonstration.

But nevertheless, is it *only* emotion which the coupled images in a poem capture? Or is the emotion in its turn a means, as the coupled images are, and is the meaning farther? Do the coupled images, that is to say, evoke between them feeling, and does the feeling, in that place between, discover something more than feeling? Bring back to your mind, if you will, that old English song.

> *O westron wind when wilt thou blow*
> *That the small rain down can rain?*
> *Christ that my love were in my arms*
> *And I in my bed again.*

There is the west wind, the spring wind, and its small rain. There is a bed and a girl. And there is emotion certainly there between them, an ache of longing. But is that all? Or is there also, and on beyond, a recognition of something known, something known before and now, in the space between the bed and the west wind, *realized?* Are the bed and the girl and the wind and the rain in some way caught up together, not in the mind, which cannot understand these irrelevancies, but in the emotion which can? And does the emotion itself change in consequence of the images which create it so that what was at first a passionate longing for that smooth girl in that warm bed becomes, in the shadow of wind and rain, bed and girl, a longing which is part of the turning of the earth and the changing of the seasons and the wet Atlantic wind which brings the spring into that island? Has this hollow between the wind and the rain on one side and the bed and the girl on the other filled, not with emotion only, but with something emotion *knows* — something more immediate than knowledge, something tangible and felt, something as tangible as experience itself, felt as immediately as experience? Is it human experience itself, in its livingness as experience, these coupled images and the emotion they evoke, have captured? And was it this that Wordsworth meant when he spoke of truth "carried alive into the heart by passion"?

In part, I should say. But I should not feel, in saying so, that I had answered the question — that I had really explained the power of these coupled images. To carry experience itself alive into the heart is an extraordinary achievement, an achievement neither science nor philosophy has accomplished. But is the possession of experience, even its possession alive, an ultimate conquest? Is it because "O westron wind . . ." enables us to possess a living moment of experience that we have treasured this little four-line poem for hundreds of

years as though it had told us a secret? I think not. And
certainly Wordsworth did not think so, for what is carried
alive into the heart in his saying is, you will remember,
"truth." It is *meaning* he means. And it is meaning we must
mean also if we are to push our question to conclusions. For
there *is* a sense of meaning, an odor of meaning one might
almost say, about these coupled images in a poem when-
ever they work as coupled images. That dead doe under
the white rushes in the ancient Chinese poem, and the living
girl who lies with her lover in the place beside, seem not only
to *be* together but to *mean* together — so much so that one's
first impulse is to make them one: dead doe under that bundle
of white rushes mistaken for living girl covered by her lover's
body — so much so indeed, that Pound, when he translated
this poem, was tempted to, and did, introduce a line which is
not there: "dead as doe is maidenhead" — with the result that
the poem is at once "explained" and destroyed in a single
stroke.

But what meaning *can* there be in this collision of images
which do not collide — images as logically unrelated as the
baily's bell, and the robes in folds, and the sun in the glass
window in "The maidens came . . ."? How can the relation
of the unrelated be said, in poetry, to *mean* and what kind
of meaning is it which only the emotions can understand?
This question, obviously, takes me farther than I ought to try
to go alone, for it pushes past the gates and doors of the art
of poetry to the art itself — to the forbidden place within
the art where the Pytho sits above the vapor. What is in-
volved is the *nature* of meaning in poetry. Fortunately how-
ever there are witnesses qualified to speak who have spoken.
And fortunately also, what they have seen and said has been
very much the same. C. Day Lewis sums it up for men of our
tongue by saying, in his *Poetic Image*, that if the poets of
England were questioned on the ultimates of their art they

would all reply, because, in one way or another, they all have, that "poetry's truth comes from the perception of a unity underlying and relating all phenomena." And one of the most French of all French poets, Charles Baudelaire, bore much the same witness in the most unequivocal terms. The poet's imagination, he wrote, is "la plus scientifique des facultés parce que, seule, elle comprend l'analogie universelle" — the most scientific of all faculties because it alone comprehends "the universal analogy."

This comes down to saying, as you see, that it is precisely the relation of the unrelated which *does* mean in poetry: indeed, that the essential meaning of the art *is* that relation . . . and the shadow it can cast . . . or the light. Whether or not one accepts this statement as a definition — and a definition wide enough to include the meaningfulness of all true poems — the fact nevertheless remains that men entitled to an opinion have thought it true. To Wordsworth, for one, "the pleasure which the mind derives from the perception of similitude in dissimilitude . . . is the great spring of the activity of our minds and their chief feeder . . ." and thus a fundamental underpinning of the whole theory of poetry which he was defending in his Preface to *Lyrical Ballads*. But whether one is prepared to go as far as Baudelaire or even as far as Wordsworth the relevance of their doctrines to the meaningfulness of coupled images is obvious. If Baudelaire and Mr. Lewis's English poets are right then images are not coupled in poetry merely to excite emotions. They are not even coupled merely to seize on moments of experience made palpable to the emotions. They are coupled to stir the emotions to comprehend an instant of the *analogie universelle*.

Why the universal analogy? Why should the comprehension of the universal analogy, granted that such an analogy exists, be meaningful? For the obvious reason, of course: because it would *make sense* of experience — and make sense of it, furthermore, in its *own* terms, not in terms of an equation of abstractions on a blackboard or a philosophy of abstractions in a book, in either one of which experience is made to mean by turning it into something else. If the fragments of experience are in truth parts of a whole, and if the relation of the parts to each other and thus to the whole can in truth be *seen, sensed, felt* in the fragments themselves, then there *is* meaning in that seeing, in that sensing, in that feeling — extraordinary meaning.

Even, sometimes, unbearable meaning. There is a poem of Baudelaire's, which Cézanne is said to have had by heart and to have used both as touchstone and lantern, which will show, if you will look at it, just how unbearable the comprehension of the universal analogy can be — the terrible poem called "Une Charogne" (A Carcass, A Carrion) in which death and sexuality are coupled in the incongruous congruity of panting lasciviousness and heaving putrescence. When you read it — if you read it — ask yourself if you think it was written merely to shock. And ask yourself too whether you think you will remember it only because it is horrible.

> *Rappelez-vous l'objet que nous vîmes, mon âme,*
> *Ce beau matin d'été si doux:*
> *Au détour d'un sentier une charogne infâme*
> *Sur un lit semé de cailloux,*
>
> *Les jambes en l'air, comme une femme lubrique,*
> *Brûlante et suant les poisons,*
> *Ouvrait d'une façon nonchalante et cynique*
> *Son ventre plein d'exhalaisons.*
>
> *Le soleil rayonnait sur cette pourriture,*
> *Comme afin de la cuire à point,*
> *Et de rendre au centuple à la grande Nature*
> *Tout ce qu'ensemble elle avait joint.*

Et le ciel regardait la carcasse superbe
  Comme une fleur s'épanouir;
— La puanteur était si forte, que sur l'herbe
  Vous crûtes vous évanouir; —

Les mouches bourdonnaient sur ce ventre putride
  D'où sortaient de noirs bataillons
De larves, qui coulaient comme un épais liquide
  Le long de ces vivants haillons.

Tout cela descendait, montait comme une vague,
  Ou s'élançait en pétillant;
On eut dit que le corps, enflé d'un souffle vague,
  Vivait en se multipliant.

Et ce monde rendait une étrange musique,
  Comme l'eau courante et le vent,
Ou le grain qu'un vanneur d'un mouvement rythmique
  Agite et tourne dans son van.

Les formes s'effaçaient et n'étaient plus qu'un rêve,
  Une ébauche lente à venir,
Sur la toile oubliée, et que l'artiste achève
  Seulement par le souvenir.

Derrière les rochers une chienne inquiète
  Nous regardait d'un oeil fâché,
Epiant le moment de reprendre au squelette
  Le morceau qu'elle avait lâché.

— Et pourtant vous serez semblable à cette ordure,
  A cette horrible infection,
Etoile de mes yeux, soleil de ma nature,
  Vous, mon ange et ma passion!

Oui! telle vous serez, ô la reine des grâces,
  Après les derniers sacrements,
Quand vous irez, sous l'herbe et les floraisons grasses,
  Moisir parmi les ossements.

Alors, ô ma beauté, dites à la vermine
Qui vous mangera de baisers
Que j'ai gardé la forme et l'essence divine
De mes amours décomposés!

There are aspects of experience from which, quite naturally and quite understandably, we turn away our eyes — aspects which, unwillingly seen, we eradicate from our memories. But poetry does not turn away from them, because it cannot turn away from them: because to turn away from them would be to betray the *analogie universelle*. It is this the censors never understand. To the censors, and those who impose censorship on their fellow citizens, Baudelaire did not *have* to write "Une Charogne." He could perfectly well have gone on about that "Beau matin d'été si doux" with which he began the poem. Neither censors nor the churches which promote censorship nor the readers of poems who find this image or that "too terrible" will ever understand the little sentence Emily Dickinson wrote to Colonel Higginson: "Candor is the only wile." If they did they would excommunicate the saint of Amherst and burn her books.

No, to see the universal analogy one must first see the universe and no man can be a reader of poems, to say nothing of being a writer of poems, who cannot, or will not, see that far. And neither can any man be a writer of poems, or a right reader of them, who, when he *has* seen, blinds himself to the congruity of the incongruous because he does not *wish* incongruous things to touch each other — cannot bear the thought that they should touch each other. Most of us keep the bones of the dead out of our minds. Most of us delight in thinking of the bright hair of a lovely girl. But the man who keeps the two so far apart that they can never meet may miss the meaning of his life to say nothing of the meaning of John Donne's "The Relic."

When my grave is broke up again
Some second guest to entertain,
        (For graves have learn'd that womanhead
        To be to more than one a bed)
            And he that digs it, spies
A bracelet of bright hair about the bone,
            Will he not let'us alone,
And think that there a loving couple lies,
Who thought that this device might be some way
To make their souls, at the last busy day,
Meet at this grave, and make a little stay?

        If this fall in a time, or land,
        Where mis-devotion doth command,
        Then he that digs us up will bring
        Us to the Bishop and the King,
            To make us Relics; then
Thou shalt be a Mary Magdalen, and I
            A something else thereby;
All women shall adore us, and some men;
And since at such time, miracles are sought,
I would have that age by this paper taught
What miracles we harmless lovers wrought.

        First, we lov'd well and faithfully,
        Yet knew not what we lov'd, nor why,
        Difference of sex no more we knew
        Than our Guardian Angels do;
            Coming and going, we
Perchance might kiss, but not between those meals;
            Our hands ne'er touch'd the seals
Which nature, injur'd by late law, sets free:
These miracles we did; but now alas,

All measure, and all language, I should pass
Should I tell what a miracle she was.

It would be possible as we all know, because we have all suffered from it, to read that line "A bracelet of bright hair about the bone" as a paradox produced characteristically by a poet who, having been designated *metaphysical* by the professors, had no choice but to invent paradoxes and other toys. But paradox surprises: it does not move. And that line *moves*. Why? Because nothing could be farther from the dead man's bone than the circle of bright hair and because nothing could be nearer. It is an unexpected conjunction, yes, but it is not the unexpectedness alone which startles us into understanding. It is the *rightness* too. The rightness *and* the unexpectedness: the unexpectedness *and* the rightness. We feel a knowledge which we cannot think — a knowledge which, for its moment, brings world and death together and gives death a place. That girl across the street there with her bright gold hair — it is mortality upon that hair which touches us. We knew it but we did not know it. Now we know.

But if the relation of the unrelated is the ultimate, or, in any case, the characteristic, meaning of poetry — poetry's "truth," to borrow Day Lewis's umbrella word — why then is not the coupling of images, which is the relation of the unrelated in practice and in fact, the characteristic means to meaning? I should have to reply that I think it is. But in so saying I should find myself at once in a distinct, and not very distinguished minority of one with the great and dangerous weight of authoritative opinion leaning above me like a cliff: the opinion of the psychologists in letters and the literary men in psychology who have reserved that central place for the symbol, and the opinion of the critics of poetry, headed by the greatest of them all, who holds (I am referring, of course, to Ivor Richards) that *"metaphor* is the supreme agent by which disparate and hitherto unconnected things are brought together in poetry." Mine is not a comfortable position to be in even in the relative privacy of a Harvard classroom. In cold public print it demands explanation.

I shall begin by trying to explain why I think the primacy of the coupling of images as means to meaning in poetry can be defended even against the claims of that enormous orbiting sputnik of the modern literary skies: the symbol. But first let me protect my flanks by reminding you that it is symbol *in poetry* I am talking about, not symbol in Jung. In Jung, as I understand it, symbols are not means at all but primordial angels, first things. They cannot be contrived by poets because they are evolved out of racial memory. They cannot be manipulated in art because they are artifacts in their own right; cores of ultimate meaning about which, as about bits of ancient metal dropped into castle wells, crystals of immeasurable meaning have gathered. They are magnets of the soul fallen like meteors out of eternity. In brief, and in Tillich's simple negative, they cannot be invented. This statement I do not question, partly because I cannot and partly because I should like to believe it true. The concept of the immemorial and autonomous symbol stirs me, and at the pitch and elevation of Tillich's thought it seems appropriate and right.

But symbols in poetry are of a very different nature as the simplest example will demonstrate. Take, as nearest thing at hand, the moon. If I say the word "moon," is there a symbol circling overhead? But suppose I repeat the most familiar stanza of that most familiar poem, "The Rime of the Ancient Mariner":

> *The moving Moon went up the sky,*
> *And nowhere did abide;*
> *Softly she was going up,*
> *And a star or two beside —*

Now is there a symbol in orbit? I don't see it. Nor am I able to see it when I intone these same lines in the most "poetic" surroundings. I say them to myself whenever, on my island in the Antilles, the full moon comes up in her harness of rare stars out of the white rim of night along the horizon and I have never yet seen anything but the beauty of the moon. But now go on a step. Recall if you can the "Rime" as a whole. Put the moon into the "Rime": let it hang there in the poem. What does it do? It changes light does it not? — precisely as it changes light in the actual world when it dissolves the familiar outlines of every day, letting that other world appear. It is when the moon changes the light in the "Rime," changes the world, that those horrible water-snakes become beautiful to the Mariner's eye, and that he blesses them, and that the carrion albatross falls from his neck. It is by the moon, in other words, that he sees — sees beauty even in horror.

> The moving Moon went up the sky,
> And nowhere did abide;
> Softly she was going up,
> And a star or two beside —
>
> Her beams bemock'd the sultry main,
> Like April hoar-frost spread;
> But where the ship's huge shadow lay,
> The charmèd water burnt alway
> A still and awful red.
>
> Beyond the shadow of the ship,
> I watch'd the water-snakes:
> They moved in tracks of shining white
> And when they rear'd, the elfish light
> Fell off in hoary flakes.
>
> Within the shadow of the ship
> I watch'd their rich attire:

Blue, glossy green, and velvet black,
They coil'd and swam; and every track
Was a flash of golden fire.

O happy living things! no tongue
Their beauty might declare:
A spring of love gush'd from my heart,
And I bless'd them unaware:
Sure my kind saint took pity on me,
And I bless'd them unaware.

The selfsame moment I could pray;
And from my neck so free
The Albatross fell off, and sank
Like lead into the sea.

Is there a symbol here? Contrast this saving light of the moon with that opposite light of the sun which stands above the mast at noon while the sea rots and the disgusting snakes coil and slide in the decaying calm. Is there a symbol there too? And is it or is it not a symbol made by the poet — by the poem? If you think of sun as sun, you think of light and warmth — of goodness and generation. But if you think of sun *in the poem* you think of thirst and death — the thirst and death of that blazing daytime light in which the snakes are only snakes and the dead men dead.

No, symbols in poetry can be invented and are invented. They are not, of course, invented at will. Mere intent will not produce a symbol even when the intent is in the mind of a poet of the genuis of Yeats. "The Second Coming" is a proof of that. There is a sense of symbol at the beginning of that poem — though vague enough so that readers, ignorant (as they should be) of Yeats's "System," take the falconer for Christ. But one has no confidence that Yeats was seeking a symbol here. At the end, however, there can be little question that the rough slouching beast has symbolical ambitions. And yet no symbol is born. One can figure out with the wits and a little reading of *A Vision* what this nightmare creature is, but following him across that magnificent poem is no shadow such as true symbols cast.

> *Turning and turning in the widening gyre*
> *The falcon cannot hear the falconer;*
> *Things fall apart; the centre cannot hold;*
> *Mere anarchy is loosed upon the world,*
> *The blood-dimmed tide is loosed, and everywhere*
> *The ceremony of innocence is drowned;*
> *The best lack all conviction, while the worst*
> *Are full of passionate intensity.*
>
> *Surely some revelation is at hand;*
> *Surely the Second Coming is at hand.*
> *The Second Coming! Hardly are those words out*
> *When a vast image out of* Spiritus Mundi
> *Troubles my sight: somewhere in sands of the desert*
> *A shape with lion body and the head of a man,*
> *A gaze blank and pitiless as the sun,*
> *Is moving its slow thighs, while all about it*
> *Reel shadows of the indignant desert birds,*
> *The darkness drops again; but now I know*
> *That twenty centuries of stony sleep*
> *Were vexed to nightmare by a rocking cradle,*
> *And what rough beast, its hour come round at last,*
> *Slouches towards Bethlehem to be born?*

But, exception made for such aborted symbols as this, there can be no question of the power of the art of poetry to invent, even in this thin and difficult air. The question therefore presents itself: what *is* this inventable symbol, known to poetry but not to religion? And to that question the classic answer is still the answer of the poet of the "Rime of the

Ancient Mariner" himself, for Coleridge was also, of course, one of the magisterial critics of our tongue. "A symbol," wrote Coleridge, "is characterized by a translucence of the special in the particular, or of the general in the special, or of the universal in the general: above all by the translucence of the eternal through and in the temporal." This is the complete definition, but there is also a more compact statement of Coleridge's which is itself a partial definition and which, being less inclusive, is more useful: a symbol, he says, "partakes of the reality which it renders intelligible."

Now you will notice — and I am returning to the defense of my precarious position — that both this briefer statement and the fuller, define symbol by assuming the existence of two "things" and, further, by postulating a relationship between them. Indeed it is the relationship which *is* the symbol. True, one of the two "things" is described as shining through the other. And the second is described as making intelligible the first. So that one thinks of, *sees,* only one thing: the moon. But the other is there, must be there, or there is no symbol. It is a mistake and a delusion, in other words, to think of symbol in poetry as Yeats sometimes did as one "thing" substituted for another. A symbol no more "stands for" something other than itself than the dead doe "stands for" the excited girl in that Chinese song. A symbol is always what George Whalley has called "a focus of relationship." Unless it is felt as a focus of relationship with both its related parts in play it will not work. It will not indeed exist. Think of any symbol you please. Think of the sign of the cross itself. You can easily imagine a context in which two lines at right angles will mean an illiterate's signature or danger at a railroad crossing. Only when that Other is there behind does this most powerful of all modern symbols become a symbol and *say.*

I am not contending, I need hardly point out — I hope I need hardly point out — that symbols and coupled images are the same thing. They have obvious differences. What I am contending is that their basic *structure* is essentially the same: that it is *relationship* here as elsewhere in poetry which provides the means to meaning. It is true that the relationship here is one of *congruity:* the invisible partner in the relationship must, as Coleridge says, be congruous with the visible if there is to be a symbol, and the visible must "partake of the reality which it renders intelligible": indeed it is precisely because of this congruity that great symbols give that "shock of recognition . . . almost remembrance" of which Keats wrote. It is true also that the relations of coupled images are commonly relationships of *incongruity*. But what is important in both cases is, I submit, the relationship, the *coupling*, and not the way the coupling fits. The "universal analogy" is comprehended in one way by symbol and in another way by coupled images. In a symbol the one "thing" is in front and the other behind. In coupled images they stand there side by side. In a symbol the one "thing" partakes of the nature of the other. In coupled images the two "things" are often as far apart as fleshless bone and bracelet of bright hair. But in both the means to meaning are the same. Both make sense of the world by showing us relationships we had not seen. And unless the relationship is shown, neither has sense to make. That gross beast at the end of "The Second Coming" is not a symbol for that simple reason: the second figure of the intended pair is missing — is not "there."

Which brings me to my second, and equally vulnerable front. Here authoritative opinion is not so much opposed as merely averted. When Ivor Richards says that metaphor is "the supreme agent by which disparate and hitherto unconnected things are brought together in poetry" he is not denying the power of images in conjunction — a power to which he is as sensitive as any man alive. He is merely saying that this power is inferior to the power of metaphor — a subordinate instance — an implicit *kind* of metaphor, to which metaphor itself must be "supreme." I am therefore not only outnumbered but ignored before I even begin to argue. And yet I cannot bring myself to submit. The considerations which apply in the case of symbol seem to me to apply with equal or even greater force in the case of metaphor. For what gives a metaphor its power is not, as some writers seem to imply, a mysterious virtue inherent in the name. What gives a metaphor its power is precisely the coupling of the images of which all metaphors are composed.

But here again, as in the case of symbol, I must repeat that it is metaphor *in poetry* I am discussing. For metaphors, of course, exist outside of poetry. They are common animals found in every use of words, including — particularly including — ordinary conversation. The difference is that in ordinary conversation, and in most kinds of prose, metaphors are only half alive, and tend, like grey cats at night, to disappear into the verbiage. They become clichés. Indeed a surprising number of the most depressing clichés in the language are precisely half-dead metaphors. They have ceased to express a relationship. Which means, since a metaphor *is* a relationship, that they have ceased to express. We say that a ship plows the sea but all we communicate is a ship moving. There is no plow. No plowshare. Nothing but a ship. And eventually even the ship vanishes into its verb.

In poetry, on the other hand — in a good poem — a metaphor is always a relationship: "the application," as Aristotle puts it in the *Poetics*, "of an alien name by transference either from genus to species, or from species to species, or by analogy, that is, proportion." Or, to use the language of a

modern dictionary, a metaphor is a figure of speech character-
ized by the transference of a name or descriptive term to some
object to which it is not properly applicable. A carrying-over,
in other words, of a name, applicable to one object, to another
object to which it is not applicable: an "alien name": a name
which becomes "alien" in the process of transference. There
are always, that is to say, two objects, two "things," in any
live metaphor, any metaphor live enough to be used in a good
poem. Let me take an example from that mine of live
metaphors, Andrew Marvell's "To His Coy Mistress":

> *My vegetable love should grow*
> *Vaster than empires, and more slow . . .*

Here the two "things" are a vegetable — my students were
drawn toward a cabbage implacably but imperceptibly bloat-
ing itself on the fat soil of a garden bed — and love: in
the context of the poem, eager, instant, breathless desiring
love. And the name of the first — "alien" indeed — has been
transferred to the second. An incongruous pair have been
married but they are still a pair and the incongruity is only
the more noticeable, like that of a small husband and a large
wife, because they are now to be treated as one. Indeed the
whole force of the metaphor, and this is a metaphor of mem-
orable force, lies precisely in the fact that although the two are
one they are still two. And this is so not only of Marvell's
metaphor but of all live metaphors. What else does that fa-
mous saying of Aristotle's mean: that "a good metaphor im-
plies the intuitive perception of the similarity in dissimilars"?
   But how then, if there are always two "things," two ob-
jects, in a live metaphor, and if their dissimilarity as well as
their similarity remains visible — how does the power of
metaphor differ from the power of the coupling of images?

The "alien name," the marriage, does of course affect the relation of the partners to each other. They lie, not side by side in the oakenshaw; but roped together by a borrowed word. But because they are closer linked do they move us more deeply and so enable us more immediately or more profoundly to perceive that similarity in dissimilars which Aristotle and Baudelaire and all the English poets agree to be the key to "meaning" in poetry?

Questions like these can only be carried to poems for there is no other judge to judge. I should like to submit this particular question to the famous poem of Marvell I have just cited.

> *Had we but world enough, and time,*
> *This coyness, lady, were no crime.*
> *We would sit down, and think which way*
> *To walk, and pass our long love's day.*
> *Thou by the Indian Ganges' side*
> *Should'st rubies find: I by the tide*
> *Of Humber would complain. I would*
> *Love you ten years before the Flood,*
> *And you should, if you please, refuse*
> *Till the conversion of the Jews.*
> *My vegetable love should grow*
> *Vaster than empires, and more slow,*
> *An hundred years should go to praise*
> *Thine eyes, and on thy forehead gaze:*
> *Two hundred to adore each breast:*
> *But thirty thousand to the rest;*
> *An age at least to every part,*
> *And the last age should show your heart.*
> *For, lady, you deserve this state,*
> *Nor would I love at lower rate.*
>   *But at my back I always hear*
> *Time's wingèd chariot hurrying near:*

And yonder all before us lie
Deserts of vast eternity.
Thy beauty shall no more be found;
Nor, in thy marble vault, shall sound
My echoing song: then worms shall try
That long-preserved virginity,
And your quaint honour turn to dust,
And into ashes all my lust.
The grave's a fine and private place,
But none, I think, do there embrace.
*   Now, therefore, while the youthful hue*
Sits on thy skin like morning dew,
And while thy willing soul transpires
At every pore with instant fires,
Now let us sport us while we may;
And now, like amorous birds of prey,
Rather at once our Time devour,
Than languish in his slow-chapt power.
Let us roll all our strength and all
Our sweetness up into one ball,
And tear our pleasures with rough strife
Thorough the iron gates of life.
Thus, though we cannot make our sun
Stand still, yet we will make him run.

On its face this poem is, of course, a speech in three parts,
or an epistle in three pleadings, or a one-sided conversation in
three *reprises,* having for end and aim to persuade a young
lady upon whose skin there still sits "the youthful hue" to
a certain course of conduct. An invitation, you might say,
to the oldest waltz. As a piece of persuasion, it is not par-
ticularly elegant. The argument comes down to this: if we
had all the time in the world, or all the world in time, we
could spend both adoring and being adored, but since we
haven't, let's get on with it. Logical enough, candid enough,

brutal enough — so brutal that one of my students (and it did his feelings credit) once stopped right there — but scarcely a poem worth reading after adolescence. Sex — the preconceptions of certain of our younger contemporaries among the novelists to the contrary notwithstanding — is interesting but not as interesting as all that. It is not, except momentarily, an end in itself.

But Marvell's poem *is* interesting — has been continuously interesting for more than three hundred years — is indeed far more than interesting. And why? Because it is obviously *not* the simple exercise in amorous rhetoric it appears to be. But why is it more? Again for an obvious reason: because it is constructed of a series of vivid figures which will not let it lie inert in the inanity of its apparent theme. But how can they prevent it from lying so? Because, like all such figures, they are two-legged creatures, and because they stand, in this poem, with one leg in the little amorous game and with the other in tragic life. Because the *time* they know, and the time the poem, through them, comes to know, is not the little hour of delay between the lover's wanting and the lover's having, but the little length of life itself with deserts of vast eternity beyond it. Because the *desire* they know is not the lover's instant urgency of desiring but the urgency of that wingèd chariot "I always hear" — which *we* too always hear when we are brave enough to listen. Because the *coyness* they know is not the coyness of that girl's refusal for *now*, for a moment, but of life's ultimate refusal forever — which is not coy.

We have a cliché we use too often when we discuss the reading of poems. We talk about "levels." We say, at this level it means this; at a second level something quite different; at a third . . . at a fourth. . . . It is a word which saves time perhaps and may even mean something as a shorthand sign but as a metaphor it is deceptive. It implies that a poem is like an apartment house: you climb from one story to the next and each floor is separate and distinct: the rooms — the arrangement of the rooms — are identical but everything else is different . . . the furniture . . . the view. One does not read a poem in this way. One does not read one's self from one floor up to the next until finally — I suppose — one emerges from the fire exit on the roof. One never leaves — if you wish to persist in a metaphor from the building trades — one never leaves the first story. And one does not read one's self *up* or *down*. One stands there and reads *through:* through the sounds, but never leaving the sounds, into their references, through the references to the images they make, through the images to their relation to each other, through their relation to each other to the feel of meaning. It is perspective one reads for in a poem, and perspective includes the near things as well as the far and includes them all at the same time and in the same scene.

It is perspective one reads for because meaning in a poem *is* perspective — the perspective which puts everything in place. The universal analogy is never seen but in perspective — in that glimpse.

And it is for this reason that Marvell's poem both is and is not an essay in seduction: because the figures of the poem open *through*. But how do they open through? Some as metaphors: vegetable love, Time's wingèd chariot, Time's slow-chapt power, the iron gates of life. Some as coupled images in which no name is transferred but things re-main themselves — remain, in one case, horribly themselves: ". . . then worms shall try / That long preserv'd virginity." Some as neither or both:

> *The grave's a fine and private place,*
> *But none, I think, do there embrace.*

Here there is no "alien name" and things remain themselves

and what is said is true, grimly true — though that grave is
all but turned to dreadful boudoir by the irony of the "fine
and private place."

But though this strange enlargement of the seeming cynical
poem is accomplished by figures of several kinds of which
metaphor is one, all these figures have in common the power
of the coupled image. They all compose congruities of in-
congruousness by placing images side by side: vegetable and
love, time and chariot, lover and worm. And it is this mating
and matching of what does not mate and match in the habitual
mind which gives the poem as a whole its enormous, dark
dimension, and leaves its amused and smiling reader staring out
through suddenly uncurtained windows at a lonely, cold and
unaccustomed sky.

How is this accomplished? By a figure which brings the
two impossible halves of the whole scene together:

> *Let us roll all our strength and all*
> *Our sweetness up into one ball,*
> *And tear our pleasures with rough strife*
> *Thorough the iron gates of life.*
> *Thus, though we cannot make our sun*
> *Stand still, yet we will make him run.*

Here on the one side is the amorous play which is the poem's
apparent theme: more than the amorous play — the act of
love itself: his strength, her sweetness. Here on the other are
the iron gates of life: time and death — time which turns lust
to ashes and the denial of lust to dust. And suddenly the two
are met. We tear our pleasures with rough strife not through
the lovely gates of love but through the iron gates of life.
We master time and death itself by passion. It is a brief vic-
tory: we cannot make our sun stand still. But it is a victory
notwithstanding: we can make him run.

True? Is it true that human passion can master time? Well, isn't it? — when time and human passion are brought face to face in the figure of this poem with death before them and the chariot behind? Is not human lust, in *that* perspective, a part of life and death and so not careless lust but tragic love? And is it not conceivable that love can master time? Is it not perhaps in that perspective that the poem "means"?

II

The Shape
of Meaning

CHAPTER FIVE

The Private World

Poems of Emily Dickinson

Having by now raised more vexed questions about poetry than a modest book ought decently to contain, and having settled them, if at all, only as one might settle a roomful of difficult visitors in an uneasy watching circle, I turn, for my remaining four chapters, to the particulars of poetry itself, which is to say, to the poems of four quite different poets. But I turn to them not to write essays on these poets: I would not know how to expatiate "on" any one of the four — and certainly not in such brief compass. Rather, I wish to use their poems to continue in terms of ends the examination of the means of poetry to which the foregoing chapters have been devoted. In those earlier chapters I attempted to discuss the means to meaning which the art of poetry employs — that relating of the unrelated which seems to reveal the *analogie universelle* by which, as poets say, their art gives reasons to experience. In these chapters I wish to examine, not the means to meaning, but meanings themselves as specific poems have discerned them in specific experiences:

the experience of the private world; the experience of the public world; the experience of the rejection of the world; the experience of the acceptance of the world.

However, I must admit at the outset that it is not possible wholly to separate means from meaning in poetry or in any other art, for the means contain the meaning. Emily Dickinson is an obvious example precisely because her poems appear to prove the contrary. On first reading there are no means; there is nothing but meaning. Her use of words as sounds is simple — as simple as the hymnbook from which she borrowed it. Her organization of words as meanings, though sometimes a little difficult, a little too colloquial or not quite colloquial enough, appears to be decipherable in the usual way of prose. Her images are so familiar as to be barely visible or so strangely abstracted as to be almost transparent. And her reader, her first-time reader, often ends, not with a handful of poems, but with a handful of aphorisms such as: good comes from evil, having is taught by having not, suffering enriches. It is only by a second reading — or by another reader — that the aphorisms can be turned back into poems and discovered to mean something very different. And this rereading involves, of course, a reconsideration of those means to meaning — an opening of eyes and ears.

One can begin with the ears. It is true that the patterns of Emily's sounds are simple, both rhythmically and otherwise.

Our share of night to bear —
Our share of morning —
Our blank in bliss to fill
Our blank in scorning —

Here a star, and there a star,
Some lose their way!

Here a mist, and there a mist,
Afterwards — Day!   (113) [1]

The second stanza varies the pattern established by the first
but the pattern of the first is as persistent and graceless as that
of any common hymn. But though the same thing is true of
the sound of many — perhaps most — of Emily's poems,
something else is true also. A protracted reading may set
a metronome to ticking in the ear but a protracted reading
will also demonstrate that the simplicity and even the grace-
lessness of the structure of sound has something to do with
the power of the poem to contain what it contains. Few
poets, Blake among them, have used words as sounds in as
primitive a way while using the same words as meanings in
a way so far from primitive. And not even Blake pushed his
organization of words as meanings as far toward the unsay-
able as Emily sometimes did in these simple-sounding little
tunes:

A solemn thing — it was — I said —
A Woman — white — to be —
And wear — if God should count me fit —
Her blameless mystery —

A timid thing — to drop a life
Into the mystic well —
Too plummetless — that it come back —
Eternity — until —   (271)

What becomes obvious on careful reading, in other words, is
the fact that Emily, far from ignoring the structure of words
as sounds, employs it deliberately and consciously to hold,

---

[1] Numbers in parentheses in this chapter refer to poem numbers in
Thomas H. Johnson, ed., *The Poems of Emily Dickinson* (3 vols.; Cam-
bridge: Harvard University Press, 1955).

in firm shapes of emphatic rhythm, structures of words as meanings which, without such firm support, might have disintegrated into meaninglessness. It is not syntax, you will have noticed, which holds the end of that last poem together: ". . . that it come back — / Eternity — until — "

No, I know no poems in which the double structure of words as sounds and words as meanings — that curious relationship of the logically unrelated — will be found, on right reading, to be more *comprehensive* than it is in the poems of Emily Dickinson. But the same thing is not true of the coupling of Emily's images, either in metaphor or out of it. Here it takes more than a second reading or even a third to demonstrate that there are images at work at all. "Amethyst remembrance," "Polar expiation." Neither of these exists upon the retina. Neither can be brought into focus by the muscles of the eye. The "blue and gold mistake" of Indian summer seems to exist somewhere in the visible — or would if one could only get rid of that "mistake." And so too does "The Distance / On the look of Death" and ". . . Dying — is a different way — / A Kind behind the Door." But who can describe the graphic shape of ". . . that white sustenance / Despair"? And yet all of these present themselves as images, do they not? — *act* as images? Where can remembrance be amethyst? Where but in the eye?

The difficulty, I think, has a double cause. First, the "objects" of Emily's images are often not objects at all but abstractions used as though they were objects — abstractions presented for the eye to see and the ear to hear and the hand to touch. Second, the objects, when they are objects, are often "transparent" in the manner of the visible member of that coupling we call a symbol.

> *At Half past Three, a single Bird*
> *Unto a silent Sky*

Propounded but a single term
Of cautious melody.

At Half past Four, Experiment
Had subjugated test
And lo, Her silver Principle
Supplanted all the rest.

At Half past Seven, Element
Nor Implement, be seen —
And Place was where the Presence was
Circumference between (1084)

Here at the beginning, before dawn, there is a bird audible to the ear as a true bird should be — a "single term" under "a silent Sky." An hour later, the full song has supplanted the tentative beginning but has become "silver Principle" in the process. And by half past seven the song is over both as the "Element" it had been first and the "Implement" it had become later, while, as for the bird that sang, it has turned itself into a "Presence" beyond "Circumference." And besides it has vanished: in its stead there is only "Place" — the visible world of daylight well this side of "Circumference."

Richard Wilbur has a marvelous saying about this translucence of Emily's "objects": ". . . what mortal objects she does acknowledge are riddled by desire to the point of transparency." And this is true, though it is not always true. She can catch that most uncatchable of all God's creatures, the hummingbird, in an image as firm and impervious as a figure in enamel: "Within my Garden rides a Bird / Upon a single Wheel." And she can go on to complete the figure in a miraculous design of words which captures the bird not as bird but as tumble of blossoms and resonance of color:

A Route of Evanescence
With a revolving Wheel —
A Resonance of Emerald —

A Rush of Cochineal —
And every Blossom on the Bush
Adjusts it's tumbled Head —
The mail from Tunis, probably,
An easy Morning's Ride —   (1463)

But such images as these are rare. The more characteristic image lets the light through either by pushing the natural object back until it seems to become an abstraction, or by drawing the abstraction forward until it has the look or feel of an object ("that white sustenance / Despair"), or by doing both together in a coupling of the two. And it is here, of course, that the difficulty resolves itself. For the moment it becomes apparent that Emily is using objects and abstractions in this inverted and inverting fashion, it becomes apparent that images *are* in constant play and that their coupling is a coupling back and forth, not only between incongruities, but between worlds — the visible and the invisible.

How does she accomplish her metamorphoses? How does she turn abstractions like Grace and Bliss and Balm and Crown and Peninsula and Circumference — the most abstract of abstractions and capitalized as well — into sensual counterweights that feel in the hand like images even if they can't be seen? The poems of almost any other poet would go down, founder, if they put to sea in generalizations as leaky as these, but Emily uses them over and over and a dozen others besides (Morn, Noon, Earl, Pod, Plush, Eden) and never ships a drop. How does she manage it? By the tone, I think, in which she speaks them — by the voice in which she makes you hear. *Decalogue* is one of her words and written with a capital D to leave no question that she means the Ten Commandments. But listen to her use of it in this poem:

To make One's Toilette — after Death
Has made the Toilette cool

Of only Taste we cared to please
Is difficult, and still —

That's easier — than Braid the Hair —
And make the Boddice gay —
When eyes that fondled it are wrenched
By Decalogues — away — (485)

You see, of course, what is being said. To make one's toilet when the only taste we cared to please has disappeared in death is difficult but even that is easier than braiding the hair and making the bodice gay "When eyes that fondled it are wrenched / By Decalogues — away." There is nothing abstract or generalized about *those* Ten Commandments. The word has been changed in saying it — changed in the voice that says. Not only has the poem a *voice* (not all poems do) but it has a particular voice — Emily's voice. And it is by reason of that particularity that these universalizations of Emily's are changed to "things." Universal words enunciated by a universal voice are not poetry. They are not even interesting. (Or perhaps I should not say "even": "En art," as LaForgue observed, "il s'agit d'être interessant.") But universal words, generalizations, abstractions, made particular in a particular voice can be poetry. As Emily Dickinson proved once for all.

Tone is always important in any true poem: it is ignored at the reader's peril. But in poems such as Emily Dickinson's it is more than important: it is crucial. One of my students, speaking of one of Emily's most characteristic poems, insisted that it was made only of tone. He was wrong in fact but right in instinct, for without the particular tone he had noticed the poem could not have been written. And the same thing is true of almost all the poems which are most her own, most intimately hers. The reason is not obscure. When a poet commits himself to the private world, to his own private inward world, to the world of his own emotions, his own glimpses, his own delights and dreads and fearful hopes and hopeless despairs, his *voice,* the voice in which he speaks of what he sees and hears and touches in that near and yet far distant country, is more pervasive of his poems and more important to their meaning than the voice in poems from the public world or the world in nature or any other world "outside." The poet of the private world is not observer only but *actor* in the scene that he observes. And the voice that speaks in his poems is the voice of himself as actor — as sufferer of those sufferings, delighter in those delights — as well as his voice as poet. If the tone is false, if the voice is self-conscious, the poem becomes unbearable as well as bad for the *actor* is then false, self-conscious. If the voice is dead, the poem is dead.

This was Emily's situation. Those of us who know a little of her life — and there is little any of us can know for it was a life in which little "happened" — those of us who know a little of her life are tempted to think of her as shut out: shut out from love; shut out from fame . . . a small, plain, spinster in a narrow village whom the world and everything else passed by. And it is true, of course, that she was a spinster and small and plain — though no one can really believe it who remembers what she said of the color of her own eyes — "like the sherry the guest leaves in the glass." It is true, too, that she left Amherst rarely — to go to South Hadley to school, to go to Boston several times when her eyes were troublesome, to go to Washington once when her father was a congressman and to stop at Philadelphia on the way back. But it is not true that her withdrawal into her father's house and into her own room in that house was a retreat from life. On the contrary it was an adventure into life — a penetration of the life she had elected to discover and explore — the vast and dangerous and often painful but always real — poignantly real — realer than any other — life of herself. Her business, she said, was circumference and circumference was the limit of experience, of her experience — the limit beyond which, you remember, that dawn bird disappeared when it turned Presence. Deprived of love? Perhaps she was as the world speaks of that deprivation, but no one can read her poems without learning that she knew more of love than most of us — knew more of what is *to* love. Deprived of fame? Perhaps. Hundreds and hundreds of little poems of which no one in Amherst knew — no one even in her father's house — over seventeen hundred in all — dropped into a box to be discovered when she died. But does any one really believe that the woman who wrote this poem knew nothing of fame?

> *Lay this Laurel on the One*
> *Too intrinsic for Renown —*
> *Laurel — vail your deathless tree —*
> *Him you chasten, that is He!* (1393)

"Him you chasten," "He" who is deprived of fame, is probably her father, for the poem seems to have been written on the third anniversary of his death. But it was Emily who had learned that one can be "Too intrinsic for renown." Learning that, she had learned more truth about fame than most of those who think they possess it ever guess.

The miracle of that little poem lies, I think, in the word "intrinsic" and in the tone which makes that last line resonant with restraint and triumphant in revelation: "Him you chasten, that is He." Emily does not always reach that height but the tone rarely fails her. Hers is a New England voice — a voice which belongs to a woman who, as she said, "sees New Englandly." It has the New England respect for others which stands, at bottom, upon a respect for self. There is a poem of Emily's which none of us can read unmoved — which moves me, I confess, so deeply that I cannot always read it. It is a poem which, in another voice, might have cried aloud, but in hers is quiet. I think it is the quietness which moves me most. It begins with these six lines:

> *I can wade Grief —*
> *Whole Pools of it —*
> *I'm used to that —*
> *But the least push of Joy*
> *Breaks up my feet —*
> *And I tip — drunken —*   (252)

One has only to consider what this might have been, written otherwise by another hand — for it would have had to be another hand. Why is it not maudlin with self-pity here? Why does it truly touch the heart and the more the more it is read? Because it is impersonal? It could scarcely be more personal. Because it is oblique? — ironic? It is as candid as agony itself. No, because there *is* no self-pity. Because the tone which can contain "But the least push of Joy / Breaks up my feet . . ." is incapable of self-pity. When we drown in self-pity we throw ourselves into ourselves and go down. But the writer of this poem is both in it and out of it: both suffers it and sees.

There is another famous poem which makes the same point:

> *She bore it till the simple veins*
> *Traced azure on her hand —*
> *Till pleading, round her quiet eyes*
> *The purple Crayons stand.*
>
> *Till Daffodils had come and gone*
> *I cannot tell the sum,*

And then she ceased to bear it —
And with the Saints sat down . . . (144)

Here again, as so often in her poems of death — and death is, of course, her familiar theme — the margin between mawkishness and emotion is thin, so thin that another woman, living as she lived in constant contemplation of herself, might easily have stumbled through. What saves her, and saves the poem, is the tone: "She bore it till . . ." "And then she ceased to bear it — / And with the Saints sat down." If you have shaped your mouth to say "And with the Saints sat down" you cannot very well weep for yourself or for anyone else, veins azure on the hand or not.

Anyone who will read Emily's poems straight through in their chronological order in Thomas H. Johnson's magnificent Harvard edition will feel, I think, as I do, that without her extraordinary mastery of tone her achievement would have been impossible. To write constantly of death, of grief, of despair, of agony, of fear is almost to insure the failure of art, for these emotions overwhelm the mind, and art must surmount experience to master it. A morbid art is an imperfect art. Poets must learn Yeats's lesson that life is tragedy but if the tragedy turns tragic for them they will be crippled poets. Like the ancient Chinese in "Lapis Lazuli" (or like our own beloved Robert Frost who has looked as long and deeply into the darkness of the world as a man well can), "their eyes, their ancient glittering eyes" must be *gay*. Emily's eyes, color of the sherry the guests leave in the glass, had that light in them:

> *Dust is the only Secret —*
> *Death, the only One*
> *You cannot find out all about*
> *In his "native town."*

> *Nobody knew "his Father" —*
> *Never was a Boy —*
> *Had'nt any playmates,*
> *Or "Early history" —*
>
> *Industrious! Laconic!*
> *Punctual! Sedate!*
> *Bold as a Brigand!*
> *Stiller than a Fleet!*
>
> *Builds, like a Bird, too!*
> *Christ robs the Nest —*
> *Robin after Robin*
> *Smuggled to Rest!*   (153)

Ezra Pound, in his translation of *The Women of Trachis*, has used a curiously compounded colloquialism which depends on just such locutions to make the long agony of Herakles supportable. Emily had learned the secret almost a century before.

But it is not only agony she is able to put in a supportable light by her mastery of tone. She can do the same thing with those two opposing subjects which betray so many poets: herself and God. She sees herself as small and lost and doubtless doomed — but sees herself always, or almost always, with a saving smile which is not entirely tender:

> *Two full Autumns for the Squirrel*
> *Bounteous prepared —*
> *Nature, Had'st thou not a Berry*
> *For thy wandering Bird?*   (846)

and

> *A Drunkard cannot meet a Cork*
> *Without a Revery —*
> *And so encountering a Fly*

This January Day
Jamaicas of Remembrance stir
That send me reeling in —
The moderate drinker of Delight
Does not deserve the spring . . . (1628)

I suppose there was never a more delicate dancing on the crumbling edge of the abyss of self-pity — that suicidal temptation of the lonely — than Emily's, but she rarely tumbles in. She sees herself in the awkward stumbling attitude and laughs.

As she laughs too, but with a child's air of innocence, at her father's Puritan God, that Neighbor over the fence of the next life in the hymnal:

Abraham to kill him
Was distinctly told —
Isaac was an Urchin —
Abraham was old —

Not a hesitation —
Abraham complied —
Flattered by Obeisance
Tyranny demurred —

Isaac — to his children
Lived to tell the tale —
Moral — with a Mastiff
Manners may prevail. (1317)

It is a little mocking sermon which would undoubtedly have shocked Edward Dickinson with his "pure and terrible" heart, but it brings the god of Abraham closer to New England than He had been for the two centuries preceding — brings Him, indeed, as close as that growling watchdog in

the next yard: so close that He can be addressed politely by
the child who always walked with Emily hand in hand:

> *Lightly stepped a yellow star*
> *To it's lofty place*
> *Loosed the Moon her silver hat*
> *From her lustral Face*
> *All of Evening softly lit*
> *As an Astral Hall*
> *Father I observed to Heaven*
> *You are punctual —*   (1672)

But more revealing than the confiding smile which makes it
possible to speak familiarly to the God of Elder Brewster is
the hot and fearless and wholly human anger with which she
is able to face him at the end. Other poets have confronted
God in anger but few have been able to manage it without
rhetoric and posture. There is something about that ultimate
face to face which excites an embarrassing self-consciousness
in which the smaller of the two opponents seems to strut and
"bear it out even to the edge of doom." Not so with Emily.
She speaks with the laconic restraint appropriate to her coun-
try, which is New England, and to herself, which is a small,
shy gentlewoman who has suffered much:

> *Of God we ask one favor,*
> *That we may be forgiven —*
> *For what, he is presumed to know —*
> *The Crime, from us, is hidden —*
> *Immured the whole of Life*
> *Within a magic Prison . . .*   (1601)

It is a remarkable poem and its power, indeed its possibility,
lies almost altogether in its voice, its tone. The figure of the

magic prison is beautiful in itself, but it is effective in the poem because of the level at which the poem is spoken — the level established by that "he is presumed to know." At another level even the magic prison might well become pretentious.

But what then is this tone? How does this unforgettable voice speak to us? For one thing, and most obviously, it is a wholly spontaneous tone. There is no literary assumption of posture or pose in advance. There is no sense that a subject has been chosen — that a theme is about to be developed. Occasionally, in the nature pieces, the sunset scenes, which are so numerous in the early poems, one feels the presence of the pad of water-color paper and the mixing of the tints, but when she began to write as poet, which she did, miraculously, within a few months of her beginnings as a writer, all that awkwardness disappears. Breath is drawn and there are words that will not leave you time to watch her coming toward you. Poem after poem — more than a hundred and fifty of them — begin with the word "I," the talker's word. She is already in the poem before she begins it, as a child is already in the adventure before he finds a word to speak of it. To put it in other terms, few poets and they among the most valued — Donne comes again to mind — have written more *dramatically* than Emily Dickinson, more in the live locutions of dramatic speech, words born living on the tongue, written as though spoken. Few have committed themselves as actors more livingly to the scene. It is almost impossible to begin one of her successful poems without finishing it. The punctuation may bewilder you. The density of the thing said may defeat your understanding. But you will read on nevertheless because you will not be able to stop reading. Something is being said to you and you have no choice but hear.

And this is a second characteristic of that voice — that it

not only *speaks* but speaks to *you*. We are accustomed in our time — unhappily accustomed, I think — to the poetry of the overheard soliloquy, the poetry written by the poet to himself or to a little group of the like-minded who can be counted on in advance to "understand." Poetry of this kind can discover worlds when the poet is Rilke but even in Rilke there is something sealed and unventilated about the discovery which sooner or later stifles the birds. The subject of all poetry is the human experience and its object must therefore be humanity as well, even in a time like ours when humanity seems to prefer to limit its knowledge of the experience of life to the life the advertisers offer it. It is no excuse to a poet that humanity will not listen. It never has listened unless it was made to.

Emily knew that as well as we do. The materialism and vulgarity of those years after the Civil War when she reached her maturity as an artist may not have been as flagrant as the materialism and vulgarity in which we live but the parochialism was even greater. America was immeasurably farther from Europe, where the arts were at least domesticated, and Amherst was farther from the rest of America, and in and about Amherst there was no one near enough to see the poems she was writing except for the occasional verse sent across the lawn to her brother's wife or mailed to Colonel Higginson in Boston or to her father's friend, the editor of the *Springfield Republican*, or shown to her sister Lavinia. But her poems, notwithstanding, were never written to herself. The voice one hears in them is never a voice *overheard*. On the contrary, it is a voice which speaks to us, strangers — and how strange we would have seemed to Emily Dickinson! — so urgently, so immediately, so *individually*, that most of us are half in love with this dead girl we all call by her first name, and read with indignation Colonel Higginson's account of her as "a plain, shy little person . . . without a single good feature."

It is this liveness in the voice that makes the curious history of Emily's poems more curious. I know no greater paradox in the whole paradoxical account of the preservation of manuscripts than Emily Dickinson's commitment of that live voice of hers to a private box full of snippets of paper — old bills, invitations to commencements, clippings from newspapers — tied together with little loops of thread. Other poets have published to the world verses which, we think, should have been delivered privately to the three or four in a position to decipher the postmark. Emily locked away in a chest a voice which speaks to every living creature of the things which every living creature knows. One of my students wrote this of the poem which begins "This consciousness that is aware / Of neighbors and the sun . . .": "The words of the poem present masses of tangled logic to the mind while an infinity of inconceivables bulges round them on all sides. But the very parts of me referred to in the poem recognize themselves and the strange contradictions inherent in their existence; each word falls into place in my understanding." This is the poem:

> *This Consciousness that is aware*
> *Of Neighbors and the Sun*
> *Will be the one aware of Death*
> *And that itself alone*
>
> *Is traversing the interval*
> *Experience between*
> *And most profound experiment*
> *Appointed unto Men —*
>
> *How adequate unto itself*
> *Its properties shall be*

Itself unto itself and none
Shall make discovery.

Adventure most unto itself
The Soul condemned to be —
Attended by a single Hound
It's own identity.   (822)

Hearing it you understand at once what my student meant. As she put it herself: "The poem opens with a quiet observation of an obvious but astounding fact; death, future time and The Consciousness must meet." It *is* an obvious fact: obvious to us all when we let it be — which is almost never. It is an astounding fact too — astounding because in the poem we cannot escape it. This same consciousness of ours, this consciousness which knows the neighbors and the sun, will one day be aware of death, and be aware of it, furthermore, "alone" — be aware that it, alone, "is traversing the interval / Experience between / And most profound experiment / Appointed unto Men" — be aware that it alone and none beside will discover "How adequate unto itself / Its properties shall be" — how adequate to that "most profound experiment." What else could you say of this but what my student said — that "the very parts of me referred to in the poem recognize themselves"? It is to "me" — to every "me" alive — that this poem speaks.

But it is that word "recognize" which points us to our immediate concern in these poems. Emily's tone is one of her means — perhaps the most effective of her means — but it is the meaning which these means attain that we must question. Is it true, as my student said, that the mind can find nothing but "masses of tangled logic" and that it is rather by a kind of *recognition*, a recognition which involves the wholeness of herself, that she can understand — that any of us can understand? And what then *do* we understand if there is no message for the mind? The crossing of that interval — a crossing none of us have yet attempted — between our experience here and that "most profound experiment / Appointed unto Men"? Our aloneness on that crossing? The discovery each one of us will make alone and for himself of the adequacy of his consciousness to that adventure — "itself unto itself"? "The Soul . . . / Attended by a single Hound / Its own identity"? *Do* we understand all this which none of us have ever known — which none of us *will* ever know if death is mere extinguishment? But even if we do not understand it, even if we reject the religious belief it seems (but are we sure?) to assume, do we not *recognize* the experience itself that speaks here — the curiosity, the dread, the courage? Do we not *recognize* that consciousness, that aloneness, that interval, that most profound experiment, that adventure most unto itself — that single hound? Do we not recognize, that is to say, the thought of these things, the fear of these things, the facing of these things? Unless we are blind and deaf and dumb I think we do for we have been there, all of us; we have lived these thoughts and fears although perhaps we did not know we had lived them until now. But now we do know. Now we "recognize."

It is this recognition, I think, which is the shape of meaning in these poems. What they give us is not messages. What they give us is experience itself presented as *recognizable* experience. One of Emily's loveliest poems, "In snow thou comest," could be read, I suppose, as a little argument for life after death derived, as such arguments so often are, from the cycle of the seasons. Actually it is a winter poem, a poem of the fear which the coming on of winter used to excite in that uninsulated century in those country towns, and of the hope of spring which lay beyond — a winter poem written in the fourth dimension of that other fear, that other hope:

> *In snow thou comest*
> *Thou shalt go with the resuming ground*
> *The sweet derision of the crow*
> *And Glee's advancing sound*
>
> *In fear thou comest*
> *Thou shalt go at such a gait of joy*
> *That men anew embark to live*
> *Upon the depth of thee —*   (1669)

"Time and eternity," wrote another of my students, "are here juxtaposed: cyclical seasonal time — winter's perpetual yielding to spring — and man's time which yields to timelessness. The two stanzas stand unconnected. Parallel in structure and movement, the ebb and flow of the first carries the reader over into the second . . . The second opens persuasively in the image of the first but moves differently in one rising swell carrying the reader with it to the brink of the unknown. Thus an experience as yet unexperienced is caught and felt through its relation to, and departure from, the known . . ."

I should reverse that last. It is because a familiar experience, an experience immediately and intimately familiar, is caught alive in those first four lines that the unexperienced experience is compelled almost to *happen.* For the secret Emily owns is the secret the art of poetry has to teach all those who serve it: the secret that if the world of immediate experience can be captured, can be held still, can be made visible, sensible, in and *as* itself it will *mean.* It is this, I think, that Baudelaire intended by his *analogie universelle:* that the world is capable of meaning — capable of meaning *as itself* — capable of meaning in its parts and in the relation of its parts and therefore in the whole of which it is also capable — that the relationship between its aspects, if those aspects can be truly sensed in themselves and as themselves is a meaningful relationship — or may be — in a poem.

This is not, of course, a popular comtemporary view, particularly among Baudelaire's compatriots. Camus talks not of the meaningfulness of life but of its absurdity. But it is interesting to observe that Camus — and Sartre and the rest — have gone on writing novels and plays and poems about this absurd life. If it were really absurd a philosophic demonstration of the fact would be the last word necessary and the last word an intelligent man would want to write. Certainly novels of "revolt" against this absurdity would be irrelevant, for if everything is absurd revolt against everything is absurd too and so is a novel about revolt. I doubt however that Baudelaire, that acid and observing mind, would have been much concerned. He would doubtless have remarked that one cannot talk about "absurdity" without postulating the existence of *meaning* somewhere and that the *analogie universelle* therefore includes the absurd as it includes the rest.

Nor would these debates have troubled Emily Dickinson. She had gone far on beyond the verbalisms to the things themselves:

> *Like Rain it sounded till it curved*
> *And then I knew 'twas Wind —*
> *It walked as wet as any Wave*
> *But swept as dry as sand —*
> *When it had pushed itself away*
> *To some remotest Plain*

A coming as of Hosts was heard
That was indeed the Rain —
It filled the Wells, it pleased the Pools
It warbled in the Road —
It pulled the spigot from the Hills
and let the Floods abroad —
It loosened acres, lifted seas
The sites of Centres stirred
Then like Elijah rode away
Upon a Wheel of Cloud.   (1235)

Like old Lu Chi, Emily has captured the rain itself in the
cage of form. Rain, everyday rain, familiar summer rain,
has been caught, held, made to turn into itself, as Proteus,
that old sea-changing god, could be forced to become himself
if his captor were strong enough and had heart enough to
hold him. It is not by *asserting* meaning that meaningfulness
grows heavy in Emily's poems. It is not by saying "I mean
this" or "this means that." It is by holding the world itself,
the aspect of the world, in those relations of the unrelated
which poetry alone can manage:

We grow accustomed to the Dark —
When Light is put away —
As when the Neighbor holds the Lamp
To witness her Goodbye —

A Moment — We uncertain step
For newness of the night —
Then — fit our Vision to the Dark —
And meet the Road — erect —

And so of larger — Darknesses —
Those Evenings of the Brain —
When not a Moon disclose a sign —
Or Star — come out — within —

> *The Bravest — grope a little —*
> *And sometimes hit a Tree*
> *Directly in the Forehead —*
> *But as they learn to see —*
>
> *Either the Darkness alters —*
> *Or something in the sight*
> *Adjusts itself to Midnight —*
> *And Life steps almost straight.* (419)

But what is demanded in that struggle with Proteus, that struggle with the world, is not only to seize upon experience but to hold it long enough to turn it true. What is demanded is the courage to turn it true. And I mean precisely courage. There is a poem of Emily's which proves that:

> *I like a look of Agony,*
> *Because I know it's true —*
> *Men do not sham Convulsion,*
> *Nor simulate, a Throe —*
>
> *The Eyes glaze once — and that is Death —*
> *Impossible to feign*
> *The Beads upon the Forehead*
> *By homely Anguish strung.* (241)

"You cannot *like* a look of agony," one of my students wrote. "To speak in a language in which both these worlds belong would have to be an extraordinary and uncommon truth indeed . . ."

Extraordinary and uncommon truth. The phrase is close to one Emily herself used in the beginning of a poem with which, perhaps, we may leave her: the last word hers.

> *This was a Poet — It is That*
> *Distills amazing sense*

From ordinary Meanings —
And Attar so immense

From the familiar species
That perished by the Door —
We wonder it was not Ourselves
Arrested it — before — (448)

CHAPTER SIX

The Public World

Poems of Yeats

T HE TITLE of this chapter makes a distinction which would not have distinguished a hundred years ago. There was no difference between public world and private world so far as the meanings of poetry were concerned down to the time we live in. If anything, the poetry of Greece moved more easily in the world of politics, human and divine, in the world of heroic actions, in the world of war, than in the inward world which Sappho knew; and when it entered that inward world it was likely to enter it, as in *Oepidus the King,* on the stage of great events — fate, city and man embroiled together. Later poets followed on that wide road. Dante took sides in the political ructions of most of the cities in northern Italy and did not hesitate to mete out eternal justice to emperors and popes and priests and public men. Shakespeare wrote play after play about kings and quarrels — and not about finished quarrels only: he even wrote about his country too in lines which, though we dare not imitate them, we love —

This happy breed of men, this little world,
This precious stone set in the silver sea,
Which serves it in the office of a wall
Or as a moat defensive to a house
Against the envy of less happier lands,
This blessed plot, this earth, this realm, this England . . .

Neither Shelley nor Goethe nor Hugo stayed indoors nor Rimbaud even — though we do not read those poems. But by the end of the last century all this had changed. Symons was telling the men of the nineties that "the poet has no more part in society than a monk in domestic life" and Kipling was writing poems about empire and army which seemed somehow to prove him right.

Our own century no longer quotes Symons but it behaves as though it should. Poets and politicians both agree, though for opposite reasons, that poetry has no place in the public world. The very last qualification for appointment to public office by and with the advice and consent of the senate — and I am speaking with some personal knowlege — is, in the eyes of senators, the practice of the art of verse. And there is nothing contemporary poets and their critics remember with more embarrassment than the attempt of the art of verse to break out into the public streets in the thirties and go marching or countermarching off with the banners.

It is a curious situation for many reasons and not least because the public street is precisely where we live our lives in this century. There is always an outdoor war to go to in our time or a huge public death in the sky or a revolution down at the corner of a couple of continents or a march-past of Great Decisions dressed up like elephants in scarlet words or a band concert of mortal trumpets and drums from over every horizon on earth. All this is out of doors and it is out of doors we do our talking and arguing and walking up and down with our souls and wondering whether we'll live until morning and whether we want to. I don't suppose there was ever a generation that lived in the public world more persistently than we do. We no longer worry much about our private souls. We worry about the soul of America or about the soul of mankind — the condition of man — the human condition. We have a queasy, seasick feeling, not in the pit of ourselves but in the consensus of our public opinions, that the country is coming apart beneath our feet or the world is coming apart and we may have to swim for it — but where shall we swim? — to the moon? — the Russians have gotten there.

We spend weeks and months arguing honesty: not private honesty — not our own several private honesties — but the public honesty of what we call, with admirable detachment, our "society." We start back in horror from the revelation that a business society, if it is a society committed to nothing but business, will act like a business society and that even the public air will become a billboard — no more honest and no more beautiful than billboards ordinarily are. We forefeel disaster — public disaster: the collapse of our country, of our tradition, of our assumptions, our hopes, our Rome, our Athens, under the pressure of a mysterious fate, an inexplicable destiny, an invasion of enormous swarms and hordes of insect barbarians against whom nothing can be done. We cry out for direction, but it is public direction we mean; for leadership, but political leadership. Look as far back as you please, you will find no generation of mankind which has lived as publicly in the public world as we do. Our dreams are public. Even our terrors are public. And nevertheless we won't have our poetry out of doors.

There are reasons, of course. The world outside has grown grittier and uglier and noisier and more and more complicated in the last hundred years and what there is left of it after the wars and the bombs and the slums and the factories, science has pretty well taken over so that there is no place for a poem to stroll but up and down inside — up and down. Also we're lonely in all this noise and rush and it's nice having something at home to pet and nuzzle when we get there — if we ever do. But nevertheless the consequences are peculiar — not the least peculiar being our modern notion that poetry *belongs* indoors — that it not only has no place in the street but *should* have no place in the street — that the meanings it makes are meanings for the closet only — that its meanings should not even attempt to take hold on politics or history.

I say this is peculiar. It is peculiar in the context of the past: poetry was never a house cat before. It is peculiar also in the context of our time. There was never a public world which needed meanings as much as ours or needed more urgently the *kind* of meanings poetry is able to discover. But nevertheless and notwithstanding, the notion persists and persists so stubbornly that it has ceased to be a notion and has become a dogma — a law which poets violate at their peril. Literary legislators no longer argue the question whether poetry *can* make sense of the public experience. They argue the reasons why it can't — or rather, they announce that it shouldn't and leave the argument to anyone foolish enough to disagree. For we detest propaganda so fervently — and for the best of reasons — that we reject in advance the possibility that a poem may still be a poem even though it have political significance — even though it might have been written to have political significance. And rejecting that possibility, we accept, as matter of course, the taboo.

But the fact is that there *are* no taboos in art. Art *should* do whatever art *can* do. The only question worth considering is whether it can — and this applies as much to the power of poetry to mean in the public world as to the etchings of Goya. The only question is whether the art of poetry *can* make sense of such a public world as that in which we live. And the only way to pursue the answer to that question is to go to the poems of a poet who has tried. The fact that the poet who tried most explicitly and most consciously in our time was also the greatest poet of the time may add a certain interest to the pursuit.

William Butler Yeats not only lived in our troubled age but lived in it in a country where the very word, troubles, was once the title of the time. And he not only knew the taboo, he was brought up on it and in it. He would have understood very well the most explicit and eloquent statement of the contemporary dogma I have ever heard — a statement made, as a matter of fact, in the very lecture hall in which these chapters took shape, and not more than a college generation earlier.

E. E. Cummings had been invited by the *Harvard Advocate* to read in Sanders Theater and his Harvard contemporary, Malcolm Cowley, a distinguished man of letters and a poet of real achievement in his own right, had been asked to make the introduction. In that introduction Mr. Cowley praised Cummings for his persistence in the practice of his art throughout the difficult years our generation has known, with the two greatest wars in history at beginning and end of our lifetime and the most revolutionary of all human revolutions in the middle, and went on to say that never, in all this time, had Cummings permitted himself to be tempted into the world of action. "Duty," Mr. Cowley concluded (and I think I am quoting him accurately), "is the greatest temptation to the poet and the worst."

The implication is plain. Duty is a virtue of the public world or at least of the world of human obligations — obligations to persons, to principles, to causes, to countries. If duty is a vice in a poet it can only be because a poet has, by hypothesis, no place in the world of obligations. Whether this can be said truthfully of the author of *The Enormous Room* and of a number of other works in verse as well as in prose which reflect critically and pointedly on Marxism in theory and in practice and on capitalism in flesh and blood is, of course, a question. But the critical position is specifically and beautifully defined in Mr. Cowley's words and not only for Mr. Cowley: for his generation also.

Yeats, as I say, would have known what Mr. Cowley meant:

> *All things can tempt me from this craft of verse:*
> *One time it was a woman's face, or worse —*
> *The seeming needs of my fool-driven land . . .*

— alternatives which do not quite describe the actual dilemma in which Yeats found himself, for it was that "woman's face" which made those "seeming needs" seem real. It was, that is to say, Maud Gonne — Maud Gonne who might

> *so noble from head*
> *To great shapely knees*
> *The long flowing line,*
> *Have walked to the altar*
> *Through the holy images*
> *At Pallas Athene's side,*
> *Or been fit spoil for a centaur*
> *Drunk with the unmixed wine . . .*

— it was Maud Gonne who dragged him into nine years of political agitation which included the presidency of the

Wolfe Tone Association and even membership in the secret and subversive Irish Republican Brotherhood.

Yeats's love for Maud Gonne is celebrated over and over in some of the finest poems of the age and in some that are not so fine but we have only occasional glimpses of the political relationship of the two. One of these, however — "The People" — is sufficiently revealing and sufficiently relevant to Yeats's life as politician to deserve quotation for that reason if for no other:

"What have I earned for all that work," I said,
"For all that I have done at my own charge?
The daily spite of this unmannerly town,
Where who has served the most is most defamed,
The reputation of his lifetime lost
Between the night and morning. I might have lived,
And you know well how great the longing has been,
Where every day my footfall should have lit
In the green shadow of Ferrara wall;
Or climbed among the images of the past —
The unperturbed and courtly images —
Evening and morning, the steep street of Urbino
To where the Duchess and her people talked
The stately midnight through until they stood
In their great window looking at the dawn;
I might have had no friend that could not mix
Courtesy and passion into one like those
That saw the wicks grow yellow in the dawn;
I might have used the one substantial right
My trade allows: chosen my company,
And chosen what scenery had pleased me best."
Thereon my phoenix answered in reproof,
"The drunkards, pilferers of public funds,
All the dishonest crowd I had driven away,
When my luck changed and they dared meet my face,
Crawled from obscurity, and set upon me

Those I had served and some that I had fed;
Yet never have I, now nor any time,
Complained of the people."

All I could reply
Was: "You, that have not lived in thought but deed,
Can have the purity of a natural force,
But I, whose virtues are the definitions
Of the analytic mind, can neither close
The eye of the mind nor keep my tongue from speech."
And yet, because my heart leaped at her words,
I was abashed, and now they come to mind
After nine years, I sink my head abashed.

It seems fairly obvious that Yeats would have agreed with
Mr. Cowley about the undesirability of giving up poetry
for politics. "The daily spite of this unmannerly town" was
a poor return for the sacrifice he had been making and since
it was the only return he got, Miss Gonne proving obdurate,
the bargain was nothing to boast about. But it is not on
this point we need the testimony of a great poet: any other
poet who had had political experience would have said the same
thing and with even greater heat. Where Yeats's testimony
is needed is on the proposition that politics is forbidden even
to the poet who does *not* give up poetry, *that the use of*
poetry as a weapon in the political wars is forbidden by the
nature of poetry. Granted that a poet *will* go on prac-
ticing the art of poetry regardless of the weather, does it
follow that his practice of his art must never take account
of the weather?

It would be hard to reconcile that theory with Yeats's
practice. It is a commonplace, of course, that Yeats became
a world poet with the publication, when he was almost fifty,
of a volume of verses called *Responsibilities* in which, as his

countryman, Louis MacNeice, put it, he began to use the English language "as though it meant business." What kind of business, one sees the moment one opens the book. It is offered, dedicated, in lieu of offspring, to Yeats's "old fathers, if you still remain / Somewhere in ear-shot for the story's end." And these "old fathers" are thus described:

> *Merchant and scholar who have left me blood*
> *That has not passed through any huckster's loin,*
> *Soldiers that gave, whatever die was cast:*
> *A Butler or an Armstrong that withstood*
> *Beside the brackish waters of the Boyne*
> *James and his Irish when the Dutchman crossed;*
> *Old merchant skipper that leaped overboard*
> *After a ragged hat in Biscay Bay;*
> *You most of all, silent and fierce old man . . .*

And the poems which follow are in the same voice: "September 1913," "To a Friend whose Work has come to Nothing," "To a Shade," "On those that hated 'The Playboy of the Western World' 1907." These are all political poems and weapons too, poems thrown like a handful of shot into the face of the political enemy. The first two relate to a municipal row in Dublin in the year 1913 which may seem insignificant and remote to some but which involved, for Yeats, the dignity of culture in Ireland and the hope for an Irish literary and artistic revival — a revival which Yeats feared would be destroyed by the materialism of the Irish middle class and the censorship, the penny-pinching and the bigotry. That his fears were grounded we now know with the suppression in Ireland of Joyce's *Stephen Hero*, the prohibition on the importation of his *Ulysses*, the self-exile of O'Casey and all the rest of that sad history behind us.

What happened in 1913 was the sort of thing that has

happened over and over in other cities but without a passion-
ate man who was also an eloquent poet to give it its
dimensions. Hugh Lane, nephew of Lady Gregory, who had
put together an important collection of modern French
paintings of the period in which modern French paintings
were shaping the consciousness of the century, offered them
to the city of Dublin if the city would provide a proper
gallery. Difficulties arose, however, over the subscription
of funds and over Lutjens' design for the building, and Lane
sent the pictures off on loan to the Tate Gallery in London
where, by a series of mischances, they still are. It was, if
you will, the familiar municipal comedy. But to Yeats it was
tragic, and tragic not for himself privately, or for mankind
under the aspect of eternity, but precisely for the city of
Dublin and the people of Ireland in the month of September
and in the year 1913 — that historical time and place:

SEPTEMBER 1913

What need you, being come to sense,
But fumble in a greasy till
And add the halfpence to the pence
And prayer to shivering prayer, until
You have dried the marrow from the bone?
For men were born to pray and save:
Romantic Ireland's dead and gone,
It's with O'Leary in the grave.

Yet they were of a different kind,
The names that stilled your childish play,
They have gone about the world like wind,
But little time had they to pray
For whom the hangman's rope was spun,
And what, God help us, could they save?
Romantic Ireland's dead and gone,
It's with O'Leary in the grave.

Was it for this the wild geese spread
The grey wing upon every tide;
For this that all that blood was shed,
For this Edward Fitzgerald died,
And Robert Emmet and Wolfe Tone,
All that delirium of the brave?
Romantic Ireland's dead and gone,
It's with O'Leary in the grave.

Yet could we turn the years again,
And call those exiles as they were
In all their loneliness and pain,
You'd cry, 'Some woman's yellow hair
Has maddened every mother's son':
They weighed so lightly what they gave.
But let them be, they're dead and gone,
They're with O'Leary in the grave.

This, as you see, is a slap in the face of the whole city, the whole countryside, modern Ireland itself with all its talk of Irish heroes and patriots, "the wild geese" who spread "The grey wing upon every tide," but with its fingers in the greasy till. The second poem on this theme is more direct, more savage and more personal. The "Friend whose Work has come to Nothing" is Hugh Lane's aunt, Lady Gregory, and its target ("one / Who, were it proved he lies, / Were neither shamed in his own / Nor in his neighbors' eyes . . .") is obviously expected to be as easily identifiable by his Dublin contemporaries as the target of similar words, spoken in the United States a decade ago, would have been to us — if only they had been spoken:

TO A FRIEND WHOSE WORK HAS
COME TO NOTHING

Now all the truth is out,
Be secret and take defeat

> *From any brazen throat,*
> *For how can you compete,*
> *Being honour bred, with one*
> *Who, were it proved he lies,*
> *Were neither shamed in his own*
> *Nor in his neighbours' eyes?*
> *Bred to a harder thing*
> *Than Triumph, turn away*
> *And like a laughing string*
> *Whereon mad fingers play*
> *Amid a place of stone,*
> *Be secret and exult,*
> *Because of all things known*
> *That is most difficult.*

I shall come back to these two poems but I cannot leave them now without asking you to say over again in your mind those last few words: "Be secret and exult / Because of all things known / That is most difficult." Public defeat is turned to secret triumph. What does this say of public defeat? — that it is meaningless? That only the secret triumph counts? But why then write the poem?

But if these two poems have to do with a minor aspect of municipal politics — for the building of libraries, galleries and museums, the houses of art which will determine the future of a city and its fame, is always a minor matter in a modern town — the third poem, "To a Shade," is an action on the great stage of national politics. It is addressed to Parnell, the Irish leader of the 1880's, who was the hero of Yeats's youth before the reactionaries of church and business brought him down with the despicable slanders which were political weapons in Ireland in that time as they have been political weapons in other countries since. And here again the poem has living figures in it: the "old foul mouth" is said to be a

Dublin lawyer who was part of the pack which hounded
Parnell to his death, and the ill-used man "who had brought /
In his full hands what, had they only known, / Had given their
children's children loftier thought, / Sweeter emotion . . ."
is Hugh Lane:

> *If you have revisited the town, thin Shade,*
> *Whether to look upon your monument*
> *(I wonder if the builder has been paid)*
> *Or happier-thoughted when the day is spent*
> *To drink of that salt breath out of the sea*
> *When grey gulls flit about instead of men,*
> *And the gaunt houses put on majesty:* ·
> *Let these content you and be gone again;*
> *For they are at their old tricks yet.*
> > > *A man*
> *Of your own passionate serving kind who had **brought***
> *In his full hands what, had they only known,*
> *Had given their children's children loftier thought,*
> *Sweeter emotion, working in their veins*
> *Like gentle blood, has been driven from the place,*
> *And insult heaped upon him for his pains,*
> *And for his open-handedness, disgrace;*
> *Your enemy, an old foul mouth, had set*
> *The pack upon him.*
> > > *Go, unquiet wanderer,*
> *And gather the Glasnevin coverlet*
> *About your head till the dust stops your ear,*
> *The time for you to taste of that salt breath*
> *And listen at the corners has not come;*
> *You had enough of sorrow before death —*
> *Away, Away! You are safer in the tomb.*

This Dublin, with its monument and its unpaid builder and
its gaunt houses and grey gulls, is a Dublin a man could walk

around in, and the dead passions here exhumed are passions that have life in them still, and the blow struck at Parnell's enemy, who is now Hugh Lane's, is a real blow which hurt — and which will go on hurting as long as the old foul mouth is remembered — which may well be as long as this poem is read — which may well be a long time indeed. It would be difficult, I think, even in Ireland where men know much about political weapons, to think of a more political weapon than this. But shall we say then that it is not a poem?

> *Go, unquiet wanderer,*
> *And gather the Glasnevin coverlet*
> *About your head till the dust stops your ear . . .*

The last of these four poems is a weapon in a different war but a war no less public: the war fought in the Abbey Theatre, of which Yeats was one of the principal administrators, against the obscurantists and illiterates among the critics, and the bigots and professional patriots among the audiences, who resented poetry in the theater and truth in the theater and above all the poetry and truth of Synge whose peasants persisted in acting not like the sentimental figures on commercial Christmas cards, but like human beings. When Synge's *Playboy of the Western World* was first put on, Yeats was out of the country — in Scotland as I recall it — where Lady Gregory's telegram caught up with him. The audience, she wired, "broke up at the word shift" — meaning chemise. Irish peasants were not supposed to speak of such things as chemises — at least in public on the stage. Yeats returned to Dublin, put on white tie and tails and faced the rioters the next night in a scene which Mary Colum used to love to recall. One can understand why as one reads the poem he made of that passion:

ON THOSE THAT HATED
'THE PLAYBOY OF THE WESTERN WORLD,' 1907

Once, when midnight smote the air,
Eunuchs ran through Hell and met
On every crowded street to stare
Upon great Juan riding by:
Even like these to rail and sweat
Staring upon his sinewy thigh.

Now no one, I submit, can read these poems without
recognizing that they exist in the public world and that
they may well have had consequences in the public world
and that they were most certainly intended to have con-
sequences there. But that fact, relevant though it is to our
discussion, is not the only fact of interest. There is the
further fact that these poems and others like them were not
written until Yeats was a middle-aged man and that his
earlier poems were as different from these as poems could
well be — as different as "The Lake Isle of Innisfree" which
we all know by heart and which Yeats, in his later years,
could not bear to hear mentioned — as different, more charac-
teristically, as:

THE ROSE OF THE WORLD

Who dreamed that beauty passes like a dream?
For these red lips, with all their mournful pride,
Mournful that no new wonder may betide,
Troy passed away in one high funeral gleam,
And Usna's children died.

We and the labouring world are passing by:
Amid men's souls, that waver and give place
Like the pale waters in their wintry race,

Under the passing stars, foam of the sky,
Lives on this lonely face.

Bow down, archangels, in your dim abode:
Before you were, or any hearts to beat,
Weary and kind one lingered by His seat;
He made the world to be a grassy road
Before her wandering feet.

Throughout the first twenty-five or thirty years of his life
as a poet Yeats was the master of lovely wavering rhythms
and lovely wavering themes which vanished — even love
itself — even unlucky love — into a faraway world where
nothing was real — where everything was made of wavering
silences like an owl's cry in a wood. Because he was a
true poet true poems were written even so, but had he died
young, as most of his friends and contemporaries of the
London nineties did, he would have been remembered as
they are — with the difference perhaps that he had attempted
to carry their belief in symbol for the symbol's sake over
into the world of the esoteric and to discover in the mythology
of Ireland a new romantic base. What then happened to Yeats
in his middle forties? Did he suddenly discover the public
world? Did he decide, like Picasso, to enter a new "period"?
Had the world changed?

Not, certainly, the world. Yeats was born into the genera-
tion which witnessed the last and ultimately successful struggle
for Irish independence from eight hundred years of British
rule. The I.R.B. was founded in 1858 seven years before his
birth. The Home Rule movement followed. He was fifteen
at the time of the threatened famine of 1879 and the Land
Wars. Nationalism became a political force in his late twenties
and by the time he reached his forties the success of the revolu-
tion was only a few years off with the civil war to follow and

the establishment of the present Irish Republic. He had never known a year when the political realities of a troubled time did not obtrude themselves upon his private life as poet. Even in 1893 when he published a volume appropriately titled *The Rose* and dedicated, also appropriately, to that archaesthete, Lionel Johnson, he felt himself obliged to justify his dedication to the red rose of intellectual beauty in a country suffering political wrong and grinding poverty. He did it in a poem which reconciles country and symbol by making them one — a poem which begins:

> *Know, that I would accounted be*
> *True brother of a company*
> *That sang, to sweeten Ireland's wrong,*
> *Ballad and story, rann and song;*
> *Nor be I any less of them,*
> *Because the red-rose-bordered hem*
> *Of her, whose history began*
> *Before God made the angelic clan,*
> *Trails all about the written page.*
> *When Time began to rant and rage*
> *The measure of her flying feet*
> *Made Ireland's heart begin to beat;*
> *And Time bade all his candles flare*
> *To light a measure here and there;*
> *And still the thoughts of Ireland brood*
> *Upon her holy quietude.*

To put it baldly — and one can be as bald as he pleases about this poem — Yeats wants to be accounted a poet of the Irish cause, "True brother of a company / That sang to sweeten Ireland's wrong," in spite of the fact that the red-rose-bordered hem of intellectual beauty, of aestheticism, trails across every page he writes. And this, he says, is possible because it was precisely the red rose, the ideal of beauty, which first "Made Ireland's heart begin to beat" back in the pre-Christian beginnings of the country when the Gaelic civilization of Ireland was a civilization which gave an exalted place to poetry and music.

The argument may not be entirely convincing to men of another country, but even men of another country — and of this country particularly — can see what the argument is about. There is perhaps no "American wrong" to be sweetened as Yeats wished to sweeten Ireland's wrong (though there is an American cause which has been much wronged and all the more dangerously because its enemies are ourselves) but the love of country exists here as it exists elsewhere and the conflict between this love of the republic and a man's passion for his art, for his craft, is, if anything, sharper with us — or was a generation ago — than with an Irish writer of the nineties, for the craft and the land seemed farther apart, more irreconcilably separated. To Americans of Henry James's generation and down into the generation of Pound and Eliot, the craft, the idea of the craft, the art, everything that made the art possible, the air in which it could breathe — all this lay across three thousand miles of ocean back east in England or, more poignantly, in France. With the result that many a young American writer or artist, and some of the best among them, chose between country and art and deserted country.

Yeats does not exile himself in space in the poem I have just read. Rather he exiles himself in time and takes his country with him. But because his solution is so purely literary, it does not follow that the problem is not real. Not all the banalities written over the past thirty years about the so-called expatriates of the twenties can conceal, even from the dullest mind, the sickness of heart which led men of character and sensibility to commit those mutilations upon themselves — those amputations of the one limb or the other — giving up the country for the art's sake or giving up the art and accepting the historical reality of the country — or mutilating the art itself, blinding it to the world around it, letting it live in its own land, in its own time, but ignorant.

No, the problem is real and has been real in every country in the West, Russia included, Russia particularly included, ever since the industrial revolution and its consequences turned the old personal world in which the arts could live in public as well as in private into the impersonal world of the mass society, and it was not resolved for Yeats by his dream of a pre-Christian Ireland. Twenty years later in 1913 "romantic Ireland" was "dead and gone": it was "with O'Leary in the grave" and he was face to face with an actual Ireland, an Ireland with a middle class like any other, an Ireland with its fair share of the hatred, the lying, the greed and the hypocrisy which afflict us all. And face to face with that public reality he found himself face to face also with the problem of art he had dodged before — the problem most contemporary poets continue to dodge — the problem of the place of poetry in this unpleasant prospect. Being the man he was he faced it squarely, and faced it, moreover, in a poem, and published his poem precisely where it belonged, at the beginning of *Responsibilities*, with "September 1913" and the rest of those political poems beside it.

"The Grey Rock" is not one of Yeats's finest poems. To one of his biographers it is nothing more than an attempt to escape from the insoluble conflict between poetry and politics by "a game like a child's." Presumably Mr. Jeffares refers to the fact that "The Grey Rock" is an allegory, for contemporary criticism regards allegory as a childish device. But this poem is not childish nor, for all its lightness of tone,

is it a game. Its implications are deadly serious and its con-
sequences are important: important not only to William
Butler Yeats but to the art of poetry, for it was as a result
of the freedom found at the far end of this allegory that
Yeats became the first whole poet of the English tongue
since Keats.

The significance of the allegory to Yeats himself is in-
dicated by the way in which it is presented — by the audience
evoked to listen to it:

> *Poets with whom I learned my trade,*
> *Companions of the Cheshire Cheese,*
> *Here's an old story I've remade,*
> *Imagining 'twould better please*
> *Your ears than stories now in fashion,*
> *Though you may think I waste my breath*
> *Pretending that there can be passion*
> *That has more life in it than death,*
> *And though at bottling of your wine*
> *Old wholesome Goban had no say;*
> *The moral's yours because it's mine.*

The "poets with whom I learned my trade" are the men of
the nineties, members of The Rhymers Club which met at
the Cheshire Cheese in London beginning in 1891 when
Yeats was twenty-six, admirers of Pater and Rossetti, con-
tributers to *The Yellow Book*, aesthetes to the last breath;
— literally to the last breath; Lionel Johnson, Arthur Symons,
Aubrey Beardsley, Richard LeGallienne, Ernest Dowson.
Yeats records their devotion to art for art's sake in the lines
in which he summons them:

> *You had to face your ends when young —*
> *'Twas wine or women, or some curse —*

But never made a poorer song
That you might have a heavier purse,
Nor gave loud service to a cause
That you might have a troop of friends.
You kept the Muses' sterner laws
And unrepenting faced your ends . . .

It was quite true. They never compromised. They set poetry above the world, making her, as Yeats bitterly complained years afterwards, "a terrible goddess" whom life existed merely to serve. And they met just such ends as he describes. With Symons it was women. With Lionel Johnson it was wine: Pound bears more particular witness to the circumstances in "Hugh Selwyn Mauberley":

For two hours he talked of Gallifet;
Of Dowson, of the Rhymers' Club;
Told how Lionel Johnson died
By falling from a high stool in a Pub . . .

To call up the ghosts of men with whom one has learned one's craft is to prepare, one would think, to discuss one's craft. To call up such ghosts as these at the beginning of a book in which the essential rule they imposed upon the craft is violated, would seem to be a preparation for the discussion of that rule. And it is precisely this the allegory turns out to be. It is a story borrowed, my colleague, John Kelleher, tells me, from the tale of the ancient battle of Clontarf. And it goes, in Yeats's much altered version, as follows:

The gods of the Irish pantheon are sitting around drinking drowsily at the close of day in their great house at Slievenamon when Aoife, an immortal, "one that was like woman made," runs in among them trembling with passion to demand that they all troop out to "dig for a dead man" —

"the worst of all dead men" "Who's burrowing somewhere in the ground." Why "the worst of all dead men"? Why the passion? Because, Aoife says, she had promised him two hundred years of immortality and given him a pin to make him invisible in a great battle between the Irish and the Danes and he had fought magnificently until the Danes "ran / Stricken from the attack / The shouting of an unseen man" but, at the last, seeing what wounds the son of the King of Ireland had suffered in this battle in which *he* fought invisible and safe, this worst of all dead men had pulled the pin out and made himself visible and got himself killed:

> "*I will not take*
> *The fortune that had been my shame*
> *Seeing, King's son, what wounds you have.*"
> '*Twas roundly spoke, but when night came*
> *He had betrayed me to his grave,*
> *For he and the King's son were dead.*
> *I'd promised him two hundred years,*
> *And when for all I'd done or said —*
> *And these immortal eyes shed tears —*
> *He claimed his country's need was most,*
> *I'd saved his life, yet for the sake*
> *Of a new friend he has turned a ghost.*
> *What does he care if my heart break?*
> *I call for spade and horse and hound*
> *That we may harry him . . .*

The figures of the allegory decipher themselves. Aoife, the immortal "like woman made" who can give two hundred years of immortality, sounds very much like the Muse who can do just that — sometimes more, sometimes less, sometimes nothing. If then Aoife is the Muse, the worst of all dead men is the poet. And if Aoife is the Muse and the worst of all dead men is the poet, then the pin is the Muse's gift of poetry — which does in fact, of course, make a man invisible to the sweating hosts in the battles between the Irish and the Danes and almost anywhere else when fighting is forward. Those lines of Shakespeare's on his homeland — have they not been heard as "the shouting of an unseen man" in many an English battle? Shakespeare is not there with a sword or a Bren gun but the words are.

But if these are the figures of the allegory how then is it to be read? What does it mean? Why, to begin at the beginning, was the dead man the worst of all dead men? Because he felt "his country's need was most"? Because he took part in the battle in the first place? Not at all. He had entered the battle with the Muse's pin and with her blessing and had served his country's cause magnificently. It was his disembodied voice and invisible blows which had terrified the Danes — and no wonder. Why then? Because he had pulled out the pin. Because he had ceased to fight *as poet.* Because, shamed by the wounds of the king's son (by the deaths, let us say, of all those who had risked their actual lives in the revolutionary cause and been executed, shot, hung) he had insisted on fighting on as a man along with the rest, in his own person. Because he had lacked the strength to live while others were dying — lacked the courage to go on living and fighting, secure in his invisibility as poet, secure in his immortality as poet, shamefully secure. Because he had chosen the other, easier alternative: pulled out the pin, turned man and died: to the plaudits of "the loud host before the sea."

You note how all this relates to Mr. Cowley's introduction of Cummings. It does and it doesn't. It does so far as the praise goes for Cummings' persistence in wearing the pin in a difficult time, a dangerous time. It doesn't so far as

Mr. Cowley's aphorism about duty goes — his pronounce-
ment of the currently orthodox notion that duty is the great-
est temptation for the poet and the worst. It isn't duty which
is the temptation in Yeats's allegory. It is the drawing out of
the pin. As long as a poet wears the pin, duty, the service
of the cause, is no offense against the Muse. There is no
such distinction for Yeats, in other words, between poetry
and politics as the men of the nineties thought there was
— or the men of our own forties and fifties. Poems also
may exist in the world of consequences as "September 1913"
exists in the world of consequences, as "To a Shade" exists
in the world of consequences.

But if this is the right reading of the allegory why is it
addressed to the men of the nineties who would have detested
such a doctrine? To justify the poems which follow? Well,
it ends:

> *I have kept my faith, though faith was tried,*
> *To that rock-born, rock-wandering foot,*
> *And the world's altered since you died,*
> *And I am in no good repute*
> *With the loud host before the sea,*
> *That think sword-strokes were better meant*
> *Than lover's music — let that be,*
> *So that the wandering foot's content.*

Which means, in terms of the allegory, that Yeats considers
that he himself still wears the pin, still serves the Muse, and
is for that reason in ill odor with the practical revolutionaries
of the I.R.B. who would have thought more of him had he
fought — and died — "like a man." But would this have
seemed a justification to Dowson and Johnson and Rhys?
Not if they had turned the pages of *Responsibilities* and seen

just *how* the Muse is being served. There would have been shrill cricket shrieks in the Elysian Fields when Beardsley looked up from the lines I have just quoted to see on the opposite page a poem entitled: "To a Wealthy Man who Promised a Second Subscription to the Dublin Municipal Gallery if it were Proved the People Wanted Pictures."

No, there is something more than self-justification in play here. The men of the nineties are being addressed, as the first line of "The Grey Rock" says, because they are the poets with whom Yeats learned his trade — which means, because he has something about that trade to tell them, something he has learned since they died, something which has changed his work in this new book. And the new book, taken together with the allegory, shows what that something is. If Yeats believes that he is keeping faith with Aoife in a book in which he attacks Dublin lawyers and Dublin shop-keepers merely because he attacks them in *poems,* then he has changed his mind about poetry since the old days of the Cheshire Cheese. He no longer believes — and indeed he said so elsewhere in bitter words — that life exists to serve poetry. He believes that poetry exists in the world of life.

What he is saying to his dead companions of those London days is something like this: You, with your rigorous standards of the purity of the art, would think I have deserted poetry in this book. But you would be wrong. Poetry is not what we thought it was when we were young — nor the world either. Poetry can inhabit the world, the actual world, even the political world. To practice it there is not easy. Indeed it is more difficult than to throw one's self into politics, into revolution, directly, as a man, as a revolutionary. But it can be done. Here is the book. Read for yourselves.

And that, of course, is what we must all do — read for ourselves. The real question about all this, as I said at the beginning, is not what the theorists of any decade say but what the poems do. If poetry *does* in fact give meanings to the public world then poetry *can* give meanings to the public world and the critics who say it shouldn't are taking more on themselves than their shoulders will carry. I should like, therefore, to submit the allegory of "The Grey Rock" to the test of the poems which follow it — some of the poems. Of "September 1913" there is little to say that the poem does not say for itself far better. Except perhaps this — that no man who has read it ever forgets it and that it has one line which stands surely among the greatest in English poetry —

All that delirium of the brave.

But does it make sense of that quixotic struggle for the soul of Ireland? No one can say who did not live in Dublin in those years. But even to us who think of it a generation later and three thousand miles away, there is something in that confrontation of heroism and greed, gallantry and superstition, which brings into focus a shadow that haunts the public world of our time and not in Ireland only — a shadow which neither the journalists nor the historians nor the orators have ever caught in their flashlights. When a romantic Past mocks a mean and miserable Present, societies see dreadful visions. Germany did. Italy did. And the story is not finished.

There is another poem also to which I called attention in a different context. I was speaking of the failure of that figure at the end of "The Second Coming" to move as symbol on the mind. Now I should like you to think of the beginning:

Turning and turning in the widening gyre
The falcon cannot hear the falconer;

Things fall apart; the centre cannot hold;
Mere anarchy is loosed upon the world,
The blood-dimmed tide is loosed, and everywhere
The ceremony of innocence is drowned;
The best lack all conviction, while the worst
Are full of passionate intensity.

Consider this as if it were an attempt — a very bold and inclusive attempt — to make sense of a vast and dark and troubled time we all — even the youngest adults among us — know. Does it do what it undertakes to do? I can only answer for myself. In the black night of McCarthyism — or the blackest hours of that night (for we have not left it) — I used to go back in my mind to these eight lines as the only form of words, or form outside of words, which could *contain* that spiritual degradation.

The best lack all conviction, while the worst
Are full of passionate intensity.

Well, you may say, it is easy enough to lash out in verse — the contemptuous scorn of "The Second Coming," the bitter irony of "September 1913." Lampoons have been written in verse for generations precisely because the verse drives the knifepoint in. What of those more difficult meanings which make *positive* sense of the public world — those meanings which poetry ought to be able to give if it has place in the public world at all?

Three years to the month after that September of 1913 Yeats wrote a second poem which was by way of answer to the first. It is called "Easter 1916" after the insurrection of that time. The Easter Rebellion was a rising engineered by a small group whom no one, John Kelleher tells me, took seriously — until the event. It was a deliberate attempt at failure — a failure which would pose again the issue of Irish independence in spite of Home Rule. Yeats, like everyone else, misunderstood it. He called the insurrectionists political innocents who would pay for their innocence with their lives. But when they did pay with their lives he saw that it was this they had intended from the beginning. He saw too what they had done: they had changed everything. Ireland of "September 1913" — the Ireland of the commonplace little people with their hands in the greasy tills — the Ireland seen from the Dublin clubs — the Ireland of the nonentities who existed to provide butts for the jokes of their betters — this Ireland was transformed: changed — changed utterly.

But as one reads the poem one wonders whether it was Con Markiewicz and MacDonagh and Pearse and Connolly and MacBride who had changed everything or the poem itself which, five months after that tragic Easter, gave their deaths their meaning.

> *I have met them at close of day*
> *Coming with vivid faces*
> *From counter or desk among grey*
> *Eighteenth-century houses.*
> *I have passed with a nod of the head*
> *Or polite meaningless words,*
> *Or have lingered awhile and said*
> *Polite meaningless words,*
> *And thought before I had done*
> *Of a mocking tale or a gibe*
> *To please a companion*
> *Around the fire at the club,*
> *Being certain that they and I*
> *But lived where motley is worn:*
> *All changed, changed utterly:*
> *A terrible beauty is born.*

That woman's days were spent
In ignorant good-will,
Her nights in argument
Until her voice grew shrill.
What voice more sweet than hers
When, young and beautiful,
She rode to harriers?
This man had kept a school
And rode our wingèd horse;
This other his helper and friend
Was coming into his force;
He might have won fame in the end,
So sensitive his nature seemed,
So daring and sweet his thought.
This other man I had dreamed
A drunken, vainglorious lout.
He had done most bitter wrong
To some who are near my heart,
Yet I number him in the song;
He, too, has resigned his part
In the casual comedy;
He, too, has been changed in his turn,
Transformed utterly:
A terrible beauty is born.

Hearts with one purpose alone
Through summer and winter seem
Enchanted to a stone
To trouble the living stream.
The horse that comes from the road,
The rider, the birds that range
From cloud to tumbling cloud,
Minute by minute they change;
A shadow of cloud on the stream
Changes minute by minute;
A horse-hoof slides on the brim,
And a horse plashes within it;

The long-legged moor-hens dive,
And hens to moor-cocks call;
Minute by minute they live:
The stone's in the midst of all.

Too long a sacrifice
Can make a stone of the heart.
O when may it suffice?
That is Heaven's part, our part
To murmur name upon name,
As a mother names her child
When sleep at last has come
On limbs that had run wild.
What is it but nightfall?
No, no, not night but death;
Was it needless death after all?
For England may keep faith
For all that is done and said.
We know their dream; enough
To know they dreamed and are dead;
And what if excess of love
Bewildered them till they died?
I write it out in a verse —
MacDonagh and MacBride
And Connolly and Pearse
Now and in time to be,
Wherever green is worn,
Are changed, changed utterly:
A terrible beauty is born.

This meaning, you see, is not a meaning in terms of propaganda. It is a meaning in terms of human life, human history — the tragedy of the heart "with one purpose alone" which, like a stone, troubles the human stream.

Too long a sacrifice
Can make a stone of the heart.
O when may it suffice?

To me these two September poems alone are answer enough to the notion that poetry has no meanings for the public world. But for those who think of meaning in more analytic terms there is another which may be relevant. I mean "The Statues" written nine months before Yeats died and when he had seen the Irish revolution collapse into the civil war, and the civil war end in the Irish Free State. This poem is an explicit attempt to move not only into the public world but into that great flow of public world we call history — to renew the Irish revolution by restoring its soul and to restore its soul not out of the Christian past but out of the pre-Christian past of early Greece. The best introduction to the poem is this excerpt from Yeats's *On the Boiler:* "Europe was not born when Greek galleys defeated the Persian hordes at Salamis, but when the Doric studios sent out those broadbacked marble statues against the multiform, vague, expressive Asiatic sea. They gave the sexual instinct of Europe its goal, its fixed type." To Yeats, it should be added, Christianity was Asiatic in this sense. It was to Phidias, and to Pythagoras whose numbers made Phidias possible, that Yeats appealed:

Pythagoras planned it. Why did the people stare?
His numbers, though they moved or seemed to move
In marble or in bronze, lacked character.
But boys and girls, pale from the imagined love
Of solitary beds, knew what they were,
That passion could bring character enough,
And pressed at midnight in some public place
Live lips upon a plummet-measured face.

No! Greater than Pythagoras, for the men
That with a mallet or a chisel modelled these
Calculations that look but casual flesh, put down
All Asiatic vague immensities,

And not the banks of oars that swam upon
The many-headed foam at Salamis.
Europe put off that foam when Phidias
Gave women dreams and dreams their looking-glass.

One image crossed the many-headed, sat
Under the tropic shade, grew round and slow,
No Hamlet thin from eating flies, a fat
Dreamer of the Middle Ages. Empty eyeballs knew
That knowledge increases unreality, that
Mirror on mirror mirrored is all the show.
When gong and conch declare the hour to bless
Grimalkin crawls to Buddha's emptiness.

When Pearse summoned Cuchulain to his side,
What stalked through the Post Office? What intellect,
What calculation, number, measurement, replied?
We Irish, born into that ancient sect
But thrown upon this filthy modern tide
And by its formless spawning fury wrecked,
Climb to our proper dark, that we may trace
The lineaments of a plummet-measured face.

As political propaganda this is worse than ineffective: it is inept. When Pearse and the men of the Easter Rebellion seized the post office and declared Irish independence in the name of God and the Irish heroes it was not the Doric statues that marched in to their call. Anything but. And yet the poem gives shape to that great European tradition of which the modern Irish and we ourselves and the peoples of Europe are all heirs — a tradition which never stood in greater need of meaning and of form than now.

But I should like to end this chapter, not with "The Statues," but with a poem in which the power of the art of poetry to mean, even in that public world from which our generation would exclude it, is more immediately and directly visible. This is "The Stare's Nest by My Window," one of Yeats's "Meditations in time of Civil War." It has meanings for that other war in which our world drags out its time:

> *The bees build in the crevices*
> *Of loosening masonry, and there*
> *The mother birds bring grubs and flies.*
> *My wall is loosening; honey-bees,*
> *Come build in the empty house of the stare.*

> *We are closed in, and the key is turned*
> *On our uncertainty; somewhere*
> *A man is killed, or a house burned,*
> *Yet no clear fact to be discerned:*
> *Come build in the empty house of the stare.*

> *A barricade of stone or of wood;*
> *Some fourteen days of civil war;*
> *Last night they trundled down the road*
> *That dead young soldier in his blood:*
> *Come build in the empty house of the stare.*

> *We had fed the heart on fantasies,*
> *The heart's grown brutal from the fare;*
> *More substance in our enmities*
> *Than in our love; O honey-bees,*
> *Come build in the empty house of the stare.*

CHAPTER SEVEN

The Anti–World

Poems of Rimbaud

I HAVE BEEN proceeding so far on an assumption and a proposition, both of which are implicit in that ancient rhyme-prose of Lu Chi's where so many roads begin: the assumption that our deepest human need is to make sense of our lives, and the proposition that poetry is one — and in some ways the most effective — of the means by which life can be brought to sense. But propositions and assumptions are crude patterns which must adjust themselves to the facts they attempt to marshal and the facts of poetry and of human need are remarkable for their inconsistency and stubbornness. Poetry seems sometimes to regard itself not as an orderer of life but as life's opposite and anti-end, and the deepest human need in certain generations has appeared to be a need not to make sense of our human lives, but to make nonsense of them. In the Dark Ages colonies of anchorites prayed for death in filthy cells with their backs to the green leaf and the blue water and even now, at the culmination of the scientific century, on the high plateau of theoretical plenty, among the

Alps of Automation, there are contemporaries who turn their heads away. It may perhaps astonish us that the age of technological triumph should have produced the Nausea of Sartre, the Absurd of Camus and a papal pronouncement that the earth was created to be a cemetery — to say nothing of the pronouncements of our own local literary Halloweeners who play trick-or-treat with the writers of San Francisco and New York — but it is a fact notwithstanding.

And it is a fact with which any such assumption as mine must make its peace. There is undoubtedly a human hunger for the anti-world and there is a poetry which serves it and no conception of the art can be complete which does not somehow keep in view that dark dimension. The difficulty is to allow for it in intelligible terms. "Revolt" has become a literary word with us. It has come to designate the work of a generation, largely French, which grew up in the years between the two world wars and which has adopted in consequence a philosophy of revolt against the incoherence of human life. But human life, of course, is neither more nor less incoherent now than it ever was and the failures of man, of God, of democracy and of science against which this revolution is declared are failures with which we have been familiar since God, man, democracy and science were discovered. The true revolt against human life is a revolt of the human spirit, a disgust of the soul, not a philosophical dissent. And to find the true revolt in action in the modern world one must go back behind this literary generation. One must go at least as far back as the tragic boy who lived the whole of a poet's life in less than five years in the early 1870's and who ended by revolting against the art itself in which his revolution was accomplished.

It is no reflection on Sartre or Malraux or the deeply lamented Albert Camus to say that their revolt is a pale and intellectual affair beside that ridiculous and passionate cry for a "long, prodigious and rational disordering of all the senses" by which Arthur Rimbaud proposed to make himself "truly a thief of fire." There is no writer in the world today, even in England with its cadres of professionally angry young men, whose revolt can be compared with Rimbaud's. Nor is there a poet alive in any country with stomach enough to have written the poems of his disgust: "Les Pauvres à l'Eglise" with its brutal contempt for God as well as man and man as well as God; that savage portrait of a woman old, pitiful, and sick, the "Vénus Anadyomène" with its hideous last line.

But it is not only the passion of Rimbaud's disillusionment with life which makes the greatness of his poetry a challenge to those who think of poetry and life in other terms. Even more disturbing is his conception of the function of the art of poetry in a revolting world as that conception is spelled out in what the canon calls his *Lettres du Voyant*. Poetry to Rimbaud was not a means of trapping the universe in the cage of form. And neither was it a means of escape from the rejected world. Rather, as Jacques Maritain puts it, Rimbaud "adhered — consciously and voluntarily adhered — to the ultimate, tyrannical demands of a poetic knowledge released to its full savagery, 'searching' for all the treasures of the spirit in the forbidden ways of a banditry heroic and villainous." These are angry words and they are angrily meant, for what Maritain's devout catholicism senses in Rimbaud is a blasphemous attempt to use poetry where the churches think only religion should be used, to transcend the word: an attempt, like the attempt of Prometheus, to steal the divine fire in *spite* of God. "It is madness," says Maritain, "to wish to have poetry alone in the soul," for if poetry is alone in a soul "which is claimed by nothing else and which offers no opposition it will develop a terrible appetite for knowledge, a vampire's appetite, which will drain all that is metaphysical and moral from the man and even all his flesh." Maritain does not use the phrase, "forbidden knowledge," but it is obviously "forbidden knowledge" he means.

It is a curious debate if one stops to think of it: on the one side the principal Catholic philosopher of our time, on the other two childish letters written almost a hundred years ago by a boy of seventeen. And yet the debate is real — and real not only because the seventeen-year-old boy was to write, in that year and the next and the next, some of the most remarkable poems the world has ever read, but because the poles of the debate are truly poles and truly opposite — and because neither can permit the other to exist. World and anti-world *are* mutually exclusive.

Even the tones of voice of the two debaters exclude each other. The first of Rimbaud's letters, written on the thirteenth of May, 1871, to his former teacher, Georges Izambard, is as jeering and sardonic as Maritain's protest is indignant and stern: "Look at you, professor again! You owe it to Society: you've told me . . . Me too, I follow the principle: I'm getting myself cynically kept . . . paid off in *bocks* and ponies . . . I owe it to Society . . ." The second letter, written two days later to Paul Demeny, a young poet in Douai and a friend of Izambard's, is less insolent but no less mocking, though the mockery here is turned against Rimbaud himself as well as against his correspondent: "I have determined to give you an hour of new literature. I begin at once with a psalm of current interest [his political satire "Chant de Guerre Parisien"]. And now follows a bit of prose on the future of poetry."

It is this discourse which Maritain paraphrases in his indictment — and not unfairly. Poetry, Rimbaud writes Demeny, is something far more important than its current practice. Ever since Greece, when poetry was "harmonious

Life," there has been "nothing but rhymed prose, a game." If Racine's rhymes were effaced and his hemistichs got mixed up "the Divine Imbecile" would today be unknown. And after Racine, down to the Romantics, "the game goes bad." Why? "The false significance of the Ego." "It is wrong," he writes Izambard, "to say: 'I think.' One should say: 'I am thought.' " "I is someone else." ("Je est un autre.") One is played *upon*, not player: ". . . so much the worse for the wood which discovers it is a violin." ". . . j'assiste à l'éclosion de ma pensée," he writes Demeny, "je la regarde, je l'écoute . . ."

What actually happens, he goes on, is that the "universal mind" throws out its ideas. Men used to pick these up letting the ideas work through them . . . Now they think of *themselves* as authors, creators, poets. ". . . auteur, créateur, poëte, cet homme n'a jamais existé." No, the thing to do is to be a seer: to make one's self a seer. And how does the poet make himself a seer? By a "long, immense et raisonné *dérèglement* de *tous les sens*" — a persistent, enormous, planned disordering of all the senses — every form of love, of suffering, of madness — ineffable torture in which he will need all his faith, in which he will need superhuman force; in which he will become the greatest sick man of all, the greatest criminal, the most completely damned — *and* "le suprême Savant." For by this means he will arrive at the *Unknown*. He will arrive at the Unknown and if, at the end, half crazed, he loses the understanding of his visions, *he will have seen them!*

One recognizes the method. Or rather one recognizes and refuses to recognize, for the rhetoric discredits itself and there is something childish in the passion like an adolescent's breaking voice. Even Rimbaud perceived the implausibility. To Demeny he defends himself behind the mask of the mocking tone. To Izambard, whom he knew better, he braves it out: "I am lousing myself up. Why? I want to be a poet and I am working to make myself a seer. You won't understand at all and I would hardly know how to explain it to you. It's a question of arriving at the unknown by the dis-ordering of *all* the senses . . ."

Yet, adolescent though the voice may be, there is something here which is not merely adolescent. There is something passionately meant and something dangerous: one understands Maritain's concern. Poetry, to this poet, is not a literary art. Poetry is the vision of the Unknown. And if, arrived at the Unknown, the vision loses its sense, at least it has been seen! "Donc le poëte est vraiment voleur de feu" — So the poet is truly the thief of fire. But what fire is this which is *stolen* from heaven, not humbly and piously received at the altar of the church? And what heaven is this which the thief can only reach by every form of love, by suffering, by torture, madness — which he can only sense when his senses are disordered? What Unknown is it which can only thus be known?

If the two letters stood by themselves they would be dis-turbing enough to anyone who remembered as he read them that they were written not merely by a seventeen-year-old boy but by a boy of seventeen who became in the year in which he wrote them one of the greatest of European poets. But they do not stand by themselves. They have beside them a famous metaphor which gives their shrillest words a somber meaning. And they have beyond them their brutal realiza-tion in a brief and tragic poet's life.

The metaphor is, of course, the metaphor of the *bateau ivre*, the drunken boat, of Rimbaud's poem of that name written a few weeks, or a few months at most, after the two letters. Here, in a tremendous figure which contains and makes coherent those earlier fragments, those dark sayings — "C'est faux de dire: Je pense. On devrait dire: On me pense . . . Tant pis pour le bois qui se trouve violon" — the whole intention takes its brooding shape. The "I" of the poem is a boat carried down unendurable rivers which finds itself no longer guided by the haulers at the towropes — the shrieking redskins have nailed them to painted posts with their arrows. But "I" care nothing for any crew. "I" am left by the rivers to drift as "I" please. Beaten by the seas like a peninsula — triumphantly beaten — "I" dance like a cork on those waves which are called eternal tumblers of victims. "I" am carried along deaf as a baby's brain, washed clean by the sea of the stains of wine and vomit, washed free of rudder and anchor. And "I" am bathed at last in the poem of the sea — "dans le Poème / De la Mer" — milky and infused with stars where sometimes, pale and ravished flotsam, a pensive drowned man sinks.

Everywhere throughout the extended trope the boat is acted *upon*, not actor. Dragged at first by the *haleurs* it is borne in turn by the rivers, driven by the sea. It is like a cork, like a victim. It is deaf. It is blind — without the eye of its riding lights. It has no rudder, no grappling hook, cannot direct or hold itself. In short, it is *abandoned* to the poem of the sea — given up to it. And so carried, so driven, it knows, sees, dreams, follows, goes ashore on, all the wonders and terrors and horrors and exaltations and mysteries: the rust of love fermenting underwater, the dawn uplifted like a people of doves ("L'Aube exaltée ainsi qu'un peuple de colombes"), the low sun soiled with mystic horrors, the blue and yellow awakening of the singing phosphorus, unbelievable Floridas, profound, brown depths where, eaten by lice, gigantic serpents fall from convulsed trees and sink, fish that sing, froth of flowers . . . "Et j'ai vu quelquefois ce que l'homme a cru voir" — And I have seen sometimes what men have thought they saw.

This is not the metaphor of The Voyage which so enchanted Rimbaud's century. Its ship is not a ship to sail but a hulk, a derelict, to drift; and its end is not some exotic country oversea but the sea itself, and its failure — for in this poem too desire fails — is not a failure to arrive but a failure to be drowned in the mysterious depth. For the truth is, as the lost boat bitterly discovers, that after all these wanderings — after driving, stained with electric lunulas, through the July storms, after trembling at the whining rut of the behemoths and the thick maelstroms, it is still homesick for Europe of the ancient parapets: "Europe where the only water one can desire is the cold, black puddle where, toward dusk, a squatting child, full of sadness, launches a little boat, fragile as a butterfly of May." "I have seen the starry archipelagos and the islands whose intoxicating skies are open to the wanderer — Is it perhaps in these bottomless nights that you sleep, that you exile yourself, Millions of golden birds, O future Vigor? But it is true, I have wept too much . . ."

"O que ma quille éclate! O que j'aille à la mer!"
(O that my keel might crack! — that I might go to the sea.)

Anyone who doubts that poetry can say what prose cannot has only to read the so-called *Lettres du Voyant* and "Bateau Ivre" together. What was pretentious and adolescent in the *Lettres* is true in the poem — *unanswerably* true. What the metaphysical phrases of the prose could only suggest, the tremendous metaphor of the poem, carried forward by the cumulative mounting of its images and the accruing memory of its music, realizes and makes real. When Rimbaud argues to Izambard in the letter of May 13 that the way to be truly poet is to be seer and the way to be seer is to disorder the senses by intoxication and sickness and sexuality and poison, no one is persuaded though some may be intrigued. But when green water penetrates the pine hull of the drunken boat washing away the stains of blue wine and vomit, taking rudder and anchor, leaving the hulk derelict in the wash of the great surge, one begins to understand what Enid Starkie means by the marvelous phrase in which she describes Rimbaud's goal as "magic receptivity." When Rimbaud writes to Demeny of arriving in intoxication at the Unknown one thinks only of certain dead philosophies. But when the helpless hulk bathes itself in the poem of the sea, infused with stars, one knows that Unknown — what it is. One realizes that the desire to be bathed in that sea, to go down in it, is not the literary fancy it once seemed.

And if the metaphor of "Bateau Ivre" gives reality of one kind to Rimbaud's theory of the disordered senses, his living of his poet's life gives reality of another. It demonstrates that he took literally what other men have only played with or rejected — for most obvious example, Baudelaire, the poet who influenced him most. Baudelaire believed, like Rimbaud, in an Unknown which it was the poet's labor to discover by deciphering sensuous experience. He therefore, like Rimbaud, attached great importance to dreams, including dreams induced by intoxications of various kinds such as he describes in his "Artificial Paradises." But Baudelaire describes these intoxications only to reject them. The poet as "déchiffreur," as decipherer, betrays himself in trusting such means as these, for the voice that cries out to the taker of drugs at the moment of illumination is his own voice and the artificial paradises are artificial indeed. Any man, says Baudelaire, who will not accept — who tries to escape — the conditions of his life sells his soul.

Rimbaud did not believe such warnings if he ever thought of them. He knew the way to the millions of golden birds, the future vigor, and nothing in heaven or earth could have stopped him from taking it. He would louse himself up. And he did, in Charleville first and afterwards in Paris. Enid Starkie's fine study[1] tells the story — certainly one of the most sordid and unpleasant in the history of literature: the swaggering bum who came home from two cold and hungry weeks in Paris in late February and early March of 1871, his hair uncut, his clothes filthy, leering and jeering in front of the cafés and the churches, scrounging drinks, baiting priests, writing *Mort à Dieu* and worse on the benches in the park; the vicious young poet who went to Paris on Paul Verlaine's invitation in September of '71, and led Verlaine, ten years his elder, on a round of pub-crawling and absinthe-swilling and sexual perversions which became a public scandal even in a quarter of Paris which few things scandalize — a round which took them at last to Belgium and on to London and back to Brussels and the *crime passionnel* which sent Rimbaud home to his mother's farm with a bullet in his wrist and Verlaine to prison. "Ce fut un contemporain insupportable," said Verlaine's friend, Lepelletier. "Il n'était nullement amusant." And one can believe him. Certainly there was nothing very amusing about Rimbaud's behavior at that famous dinner of the Vilains Bonshommes where the respected figures of contemporary French poetry were gathered — Banville, Heredia, Coppée — and where Rimbaud, present as Verlaine's guest, punctuated the reading of a poem of Aicard's by ejaculating *merde* after every rhyme and attacked with Verlaine's sword cane an indignant *convive* who tried to silence him.

But the writers who saw Rimbaud in Paris in the winter of

[1] *Arthur Rimbaud* (Norton, 1947).

1871 and 1872 were not only infuriated by him, they were troubled also. ". . . a most alarming poet," wrote Léon Valade, "big hands, big feet, a completely babyish face like that of a child of thirteen, deep blue eyes! Such is the boy whose imagination is a compound of great power and undreamed-of corruption, who has fascinated and terrified all our friends . . . Satan among the doctors!" What fascinated and terrified them all was not merely the brutality of this provincial boy with the baby face and the deep blue eyes — "yeux de myosotis" — but the corruption and, above all, the power of his imagination. They felt the force in him, the intelligence, the will. And it was these qualities quite as much as the contradiction between his viciousness and his girl's complexion which frightened them. The corruption, they realized, was of his own choice and that realization made his obscenities at once more and less despicable. He was not the victim of his vices but their inventor: "Satan among the doctors" — the young Satan.

This was the crucial realization and it still is. Everything that is known of Rimbaud's life and everything that remains of the poems written before he went to Paris in September of 1871 indicates that the homosexual, the pub-crawler and the *voyou* whom Valade and Lepelletier and the rest of their contemporaries knew was a deliberately fabricated character: a character as deliberately fabricated as the improbable "seer" of the *Lettres du Voyant*. Homosexuality takes curious forms but it is not easy to picture to one's self a truly perverted man who could write "Première Soirée" or "A la Musique" with those last lines which might be paraphrased:

> *I, I follow the brisk girls under the chestnut trees:*
> *They know it well enough and turn laughing, their*
> *eyes full of indiscreet things.*

I don't say a word, I keep looking at the flesh of their
white necks in the tangles of hair: I follow the
divine back under the flimsy dresses down from
the shoulders' curve.

Soon I have hunted out their little shoes, their
stockings . . . Burning with lovely fevers I imagine their
bodies. They think I am drôle and talk to each other
in low voices . . . and my brutal desires hang upon their
lips.

There are other poems on the same theme and the author of
none of them is Verlaine's lover. This is a paraphrase of "Au
Cabaret-Vert":

For eight days I had worn out my shoes on the road
metal. I walked into Charleroi. At the Cabaret-Vert
I ordered tartines de beurre et du jambon — those
little crisp buttered slices of bread with ham half
cold, half warm.

I was happy and stuck my legs out under the green
table and looked at the naïve little pictures
embroidered in the upholstery — and it was adorable
when the girl with the enormous breasts and the
lively eyes

— it would take more than a kiss to frighten a girl
like that — came laughing in bringing me the
buttered tartines and the tepid ham on a colored
plate,

pink and white ham perfumed with a garlic clove,
and filled the immense beer-mug with its foam
which a ray of late sunlight gilded.

And if Rimbaud was not a pederast by glandular mischance,
no more was he a *voyou* by nature. As a child he "sweated

obedience," to use his own phrase in "Les Poëtes de Sept Ans," and the year before Léon Valade saw him as a young Satan he had dutifully won all the prizes of the Concours Académique of the Republic, marching home from school with his academy medal, his pasteboard laurel wreaths and his red morocco prize books to the applause of the burghers of Charleville. Even when, a few months after that triumph, he ran away from home and the iron-willed peasant woman who had borne him, it was not as a bum that he walked the Belgian roads with the war of 1870 in the towns and fields around him:

> *I went off, fists in my torn pockets, my overcoat*
> *unreal too — I went off under the sky, Muse, and I*
> *was yours: Oh, la, la, what splendid love affairs I*
> *dreamed of!*

> *There was a great hole in my one pair of pants —*
> *Tom Thumb the dreamer I was as I went along shelling*
> *rhymes like peas, my inn at the Great Bear and my*
> *stars in the sky with their soft frou-frou — their*
> *soft rustling —*

> *And I heard them, sitting there at the side of the*
> *road those good September evenings, feeling the*
> *dew on my forehead like a strong wine;*

> *and rhyming away among the fantastic shadows*
> *I snapped the elastics of my broken shoes like lyres,*
> *one foot against my heart.*

It is usually said that these poems are derivative and indeed Rimbaud himself disowned them after the *Lettres du Voyant*, but the portrait they paint of their author is not derivative. A feel of the world cannot be borrowed from someone else. And the feel of the world which comes

through such a poem as "Roman," written in September of
1870, is far indeed from the savage disgust, the bitter rejection,
which the blue-eyed boy of the Boul' Miche dragged behind
him:

I

You aren't very serious at seventeen.
Some fine evening, to hell with the bocks and the
lemonade and the flashy cafés with their glittering
windowpanes. You walk out under the green lime trees
on the promenade.

The lime trees smell good in those June evenings!
Sometimes the air is so soft that you close your eyelids;
the wind heavy with sounds — the town isn't far off —
smells of grapevines and beer . . .

II

Look, you see a tiny handkerchief of dark blue sky
framed by a little branch and pierced by a wicked
star, little and altogether white, which drowns with
a sweet shudder . . .

June night! Seventeen! You get yourself drunk.
The sap is champagne and goes to your head . . .
You wander; you feel a kiss on your lips which
palpitates there like a little animal . . .

III

Your crazy heart does a Robinson Crusoe across all
the novels when in the light of a pale street lamp
a young girl goes by with little charming airs
under the shadow of the terrifying coat collar
of her father

and because she thinks you immensely simple she turns
with a quick movement while all the time her little boots
trot on . . . and the tune you were whistling dies on
your lips . . .

Whether or not Rimbaud succeeded in disordering all his senses by the abuse to which he subjected them in the following year, there can be no question but that he changed — deliberately and willfully changed — his nature, or at least the face his nature showed. Years afterward, his employer at Aden on the Red Sea spoke of his "mask": "He never learned," said Bardey, "to discard that malicious and nevertheless pathetic mask which concealed, beneath its sarcasm, the true qualities of his heart."

And neither can there be any question but that this deliberate change was a change contrived for the sake of poetry — for the sake of what Rimbaud believed poetry to be — the theft of fire. There has been much discussion of the private reasons for this deliberate perversion of a life. Was it the harshness of Rimbaud's mother? Was it the War of 1870 and the occupation of Charleville with the closing of the schools and the departure of Izambard? Was it possibly the reading of books on the occult? Was it adolescent boredom aggravated by the boredom of a world? Was it the failure of the Commune and the horrors of the winter months of '71? The possibilities of speculation are numerous but they remain possibilities and more or less irrelevant besides, for the true explanation is available to anyone who is willing to accept it. It is spelled out in the *Lettres* and stated in "Bateau Ivre." What is worth living for is not the world, the familiar, the near, the stale, the human, the political — "Europe of the ancient parapets" — those cargo ships and men-of-war and prison hulks of the end of "Bateau Ivre." What is worth living for is the Unworld, the starry archipelagos, the millions of golden birds, the future Vigor. And the way to these ends is by the Poem of the Sea — to be bathed in it — to lose one's self and find.

The real "question of Rimbaud," in other words, is not the autobiographical question. The real question is the question of poetry. Is poetry a power of such a nature that if a man worthy of it, a man capable of it, as Rimbaud surely was, will give himself to it, sacrifice to it (like a medium in her trance) his consciousness, his identity, it will lift him to the Unknown, to Prometheus' fire? Is poetry a sea which will fling the man who surrenders himself to it — lets it drive him, drown him — ashore at last upon the world beyond the world, the world against the world?

This is the real question for us who face these astonishing poems now. It is the real question for Maritain who dismisses it with the anger of a dogmatic belief challenged by a denial which does not so much deny as ignore: "It is a madness to wish to have poetry alone in the soul . . ." It was the real question for Rimbaud too at the end of his brief poet's life before he turned away from literature, and turned away from Europe, and wandered off into the countries of the East and of the Red Sea and of Africa to devote to trading and gunrunning and the counting of pennies, those icy, untiring, contemptuous energies which had terrified Verlaine's friends. In *A Season in Hell*, [2] which Rimbaud dates "April–August 1873," the bitterest indictment levelled by the eighteen-year-old boy against himself is precisely this indictment — that he had attempted to make his way to truth, to power over truth, by poetry and that he had deceived himself, that he was a fool.

The mockery is all the more bitter because the pretensions

---

[2] French Ph.D. theses since the second world war have argued on graphological and verbal grounds that *Une Saison en Enfer* is not Rimbaud's "farewell to literature" as had previously been supposed but was actually written before the *Illuminations*. Miss Enid Starkie, in her Zaharoff Lecture on Rimbaud published by the Oxford University Press in 1954, examines the evidence and is not impressed. In addition to her persuasive arguments there is the fact that, although the so-called "Prose Illuminations" are not quoted in the *Saison*, certain of their most striking images are cited as examples of the hallucination with which Rimbaud charges himself.

— or what now appear to him to be pretensions — had been
so overweening. "I am going to unveil all the mysteries,"
he says in the *Saison*, "religious or natural, death, birth, past,
future, cosmogony, nothingness. Listen!" "I have all the
talents! There is no one here and there is someone. Do you
want Negro songs, the dances of houris? Do you want me
to disappear, to dive to recover The Ring? Do you? I will
make gold . . . I will accomplish cures . . ." "And let us
think of me. I have the good fortune to suffer no longer.
My life was only sweet follies: it is regrettable." "Bah! Every
imaginable grimace!" And he breaks off to present Verlaine
as the "foolish virgin" protesting to the "divine spouse"
against the cruelties and the wickedness of Rimbaud as the
"infernal spouse."

But in a few paragraphs he is back again: "Here, the history
of one of my follies." He describes his triumphs with a
brutal sneer: he had invented the colors of the vowels, he
had regulated the form and movement of each consonant,
he flattered himself that he had invented, with instinctive
rhythms, a poetic language accessible one day or the other to all
the senses — and he adds, with a cackle of derision, "I re-
served the rights of translation." He had accustomed himself,
he goes on, to simple hallucination: he saw a factory as a
mosque, carriages on the roads of the sky, a salon at the bottom
of a lake, "une école de tambours faite par des anges." Then
he had explained his "magic sophisms" by the hallucination of
words and finished by finding sacred the disorder of his spirit.
He had said good-by to the world in a kind of romances —
and he copies out one of his little seeming-simple songs, the
"Song of the Highest Tower." He had come to love the
desert, burned fields; had dragged himself through stinking
alleys, offered himself to the sun, the god of fire, to destroy,
and the town with him, by a bombardment of blocks of dry

earth — and he copies out another of his poems, called origi-
nally "Fêtes de la Faim": "If I hunger for anything it is only
for earth and stones. I break my fast always on air, rock,
coals, iron . . ."

And so he comes to his "triumph." He had lived at last like
a sparkle of gold in the blaze of light that is *nature* — and
he adds: "In joy I adopted an idiot expression." He had been
"damned by the rainbow," Happiness was his fatality, his
remorse, his worm. "Happiness! Its tooth, sweet as death,
warned me at cockcrow — *ad matutinum* — at the *Christus
venit* — in the most somber cities."

All of which leads him to his confession — but not at all
to the confession his sister Isabelle wanted so much to believe
he had uttered, the confession of sin. Rimbaud's was a more
difficult confession by far: the confession of stupidity. "I
created all the festivals, all the triumphs, all the dramas.
I tried to invent new flowers, new stars, new flesh, new
tongues. I thought to attain supernatural powers. All right!
Let me bury my imagination and my memories! Une belle
gloire d'artiste . . ."

"I! I who called myself a wizard or an angel free from
every rule of morality — I am brought back to earth with a
job to look for and dirty reality to embrace! Peasant!" He
throws the word in his own face. What was he, after all the
proud brags and the insolent words and the soaring visions
— he who had seen in the sky endless beaches covered with
white nations in joy — what was he but a peasant, a peasant's
child, "seated among broken pots and nettles at the bottom of
a leprous wall eaten by the sun" — the wall of his peasant
mother's farmhouse at Roche! "Enfin, je demanderai pardon
pour m'être nourri de mensonge. Et allons." Finally, I will
beg pardon for having fed myself on lies.

Had he fed himself on lies? That is a question which was

not answered for the rest of us against the leprous wall at Roche or in the quarries of Cyprus or at Aden or Harrar or in the Ogaden or in the hospital at Marseilles where, a few weeks after his thirty-seventh birthday, Rimbaud died. For the poems of those "insolent words" and "soaring visions" remain, the poems of the "instinctive rhythms" in which Rimbaud once believed he had "attained supernatural powers" — *Les Illuminations,* as Verlaine called them when he published them in a magazine called *La Vogue* five years before Rimbaud's death and at a time when no one in Paris knew or much cared whether he was alive or not. The *Illuminations* remain and they still return an ambiguous and mocking silence to the man who reads them and says, Fool!

Not that they leave any doubt of the overweening pretensions which Rimbaud found in them looking back. The *Illuminations* are not visionary poems of the sort with which literature is elsewhere familiar — *descriptions* of visions, recollections of visions, accounts of visions. They *are* the visions themselves: the images and rhythms and dislocations in which the visions present themselves. They are actions, poetic actions, moving with the timeless, effortless rapidity of the vision itself, not the ordered time, the rationalized time, of the vision remembered. Their end and aim is the end and aim of *vision* — to *see* the unseeable: not the end and aim of *literature* — to represent it. Take what is perhaps the most "visible" of them all: "Mystique" — that little knoll opposite us where the angels whirl their woolen robes in an herbage of steel and emerald, and meadows of flame leap up toward the summit of the little hill, and the muck of the ridge off to the left is trampled by all the homicides and battles where the disastrous noises trace their curve, and on the right, behind the ridge, is the line of orients and progress, and the band at the top of the picture is made up of the revolving, leaping hums of sea shells and human nights and on this side of the slope against our faces the flowery softness of stars and sky and all the rest descends as from a basket leaving the abyss below us flowery and blue.

One recognizes these images for what they are. This is vision in action, vision itself, vision pressing beyond the limits of the seen toward that unseen which this gesturing world appears so often to promise us — the meaning beyond the means. Why, rereading this, did Rimbaud call himself a fool? Because it fails to reach the unseen it looks toward? Because it does *not* set us ashore upon the starry archipelagos, the unbelievable Floridas? Because it leaves us not with the stolen fire but only with the dying embers of an earthly sunset fading into stars and night?

Or consider "A Une Raison" which is less vision than evocation but which calls out in the live and troubling voice of one who himself *sees* what he calls to:

One stroke of your finger on the drum discharges all the sounds and begins the new harmony.

One step of your feet is the calling up of new men and their marching off.

You turn your head away from us: the new love. You turn your head back to us: the new love.

"Change our fate, crush our scourges beginning with the scourge of time," these children cry to you.

"Raise up somewhere, anywhere, the substance of our fortunes and our prayers," we beseech you.

Arrived from always you will go away everywhere.

This is true evocation. Nowhere, perhaps, in the literature of magic or of religion is there a spell more subtle than the spell of

that first sentence or of the last. But does this unnamed Being,
this Reason, appear? Or do we hear only the human voice
that cries to it?

Or, finally, read "Après le Déluge" which is neither vision-
ary scene nor evocation but a narrative, or what purports to
be a narrative:

As soon as the idea of the Deluge had abated a rabbit stopped
in the clover and the swinging bell-flowers and said his
prayers through the spider's web to the rainbow, and the
flowers were already looking around — but, Oh, the pre-
cious stones were hiding themselves. Then market stalls
were set up in the dirty main street and the boats were
draggd down to the sea which ran steeply up, the way it
does in old prints, and blood flowed at Blue Beard's — in
the slaughter houses, in the circuses, where God's seal
blanched the windows. Blood and milk flowed. Beavers
built. Glasses of coffee smoked in the little bars. Children
in mourning in the big house where window panes still
dripped looked at marvellous picture books. A door banged
and the little boy waved his arms in the village square in
the burst of showery rain to the comprehension of the
weather vanes and of all the cocks on all the steeples.
Madame Somebody set up a piano in the Alps. Mass and
first communion were celebrated at the hundred thousand
altars of the cathedral. Caravans set out and the Hotel
Splendide was erected in the ice and chaos of the Polar
night. And ever since that time the moon has heard jackals
howling across the deserts of thyme — and eclogues in
wooden shoes grunting in the orchard. Then in the violet
and budding forest the white lily told me it was spring.
Gush pond! Froth, pour through the woods, roll over the
bridge! Black palls and organs, lightning and thunder, rise
and roll! Waters and sorrows, rise and let loose the floods
again. Because, since the floods were dispersed — Oh, the
precious stones burying themselves and the flowers open! —

since then it is a bore! And the Queen, the Witch, who fires
her embers in the earthen pot, never wants to tell us what she
knows — what we do not know.

Here the difference between Rimbaud's visionary poems
and the more familiar visionary poems of, say, Wordsworth is
obvious. Where Wordsworth, dealing with a similar theme in
the ode on "Intimations of Immortality from Recollections
of Early Childhood," *describes* those childhood certainties
which later grow uncertain and stale, Rimbaud *lives* them.
Where Wordsworth writes:

> *There was a time when meadow, grove and stream*
> *The earth and every common sight*
> *To me did seem*
> *Apparelled in celestial light,*
> *The glory and the freshness of a dream.*
> *It is not now as it hath been of yore . . .*

where Wordsworth *writes*, Rimbaud's rabbit says his prayers
to the rainbow through the spider's web — and Madame
Somebody sets up a piano in the Alps. Where Wordsworth
asserts the moment of insight and tells us what the insight was
— "Our birth is but a sleep and a forgetting" — Rimbaud
evokes the actual images in which the insight exists: on one
side the rabbit and the web and on the other the dirty stalls
and the blood in the slaughterhouses and Mass at the hundred
thousand altars.

These *Illuminations* are thus, in intention and in means,
labors bolder even than the spiritual banditry of which Mari-
tain accuses their author: labors bolder than the leap of Icarus.
But do they succeed in the only terms possible to them — their
own — or does Icarus fall among the potsherds and the nettles
of the farmyard at Roche? Does "Après le Déluge" actually

steal those precious stones and bring them to us in its Prometheus sack? Does the stroke of that finger in "A Une Raison" discharge in fact all the sounds, and do we *hear* that new harmony? Do we *feel* the flowery softness of the stars spill from the basket of the sky against our faces in "Mystique" explaining everything — those homicides, those battles? Are these poems, in other words, more than poems? Are they spells to take us to the world beyond — to bring what lies beyond us back? Are they revelations of the *other* Truth — that Truth mankind has always thought was hidden somewhere farther off behind the indifference of the universe and the sordidness and misery and meaningless disasters of our human lot — behind them and against them? Or are they, after all, still poems and no more than poems — whatever poems are?

No reader of the *Illuminations* can answer that question for any other. Paul Claudel, to take the most famous example, always affirmed that Rimbaud had converted him to Catholicism and since he could scarcely have had "Les Premières Communions" in mind ("Christ! O Christ, éternel voleur des énergies") he may well have been thinking of the *Illuminations*. I can only testify for myself that the *Illuminations* are not revelations for me. I am not, reading them, the recipient of the gift of stolen fire. I am the recipient only of the gift of poetry — and, for me, it is enough.

For poetry is not revelation and has no need to pretend it is. Poetry is art and does what art can do — which is, as Lu Chi said, to trap heaven *and* earth in the cage of form. Nothing proves that more conclusively than these poems of Rimbaud which, failing for the man who wrote them as instruments of vision, succeed for all who read them as poems of the farthest experience of man. If they do not make the Unknown known they make the man who seeks it the heroic and the tragic figure which he truly is between these memories and skies.

And as for the failure, there is one word to be added to the judgment which Rimbaud passed on himself. Even in the face of defeat he never pulled down the flag of his conviction. "It is necessary to be absolutely modern. No canticles. Hold to the step you have gained. Sore night. The dried blood smokes on my face and I have nothing at my back but this horrible bush!" . . . And there is a word to be said about that conviction too. Rimbaud's anti-world was not a rejection of the *possibility* of world. Where the leaders of the contemporary literary revolt make existence itself "absurd" in its "given, unjustifiable, primordial quality" as Sartre does,[3] or derive the meaning of existence "from an original denial of the possibility of meaning" as John Cruikshank puts it in his recent book on Camus, Rimbaud cries out in his *Season in Hell:* "Slaves, let us not curse life." "Esclaves, ne maudissons pas la vie." Rimbaud believed in the possibility of meaning as any man must who struggles to find life meaningful — which means, as any poet must — and he ends the *Saison*, after all the defeat and humiliation, with these words: "It shall be lawful to me to possess the truth in one body and one soul."

[3] *Paru*, December, 1945, cited by John Cruikshank in *Albert Camus* (Oxford, 1959).

CHAPTER EIGHT

The Arable World

Poems of Keats

THAT Rimbaud's conception of the power of poetry was ignorant, presumptuous and overweening, our time will cheerfully agree. One doesn't arrive at the Unknown "on the viewless wings of Poesy" in this day and age: one arrives by science. Rimbaud learned that at the end and had the decency to say so: " 'Nothing is vanity; science and forward,' cries the modern Ecclesiastes, meaning *everybody*." It had been madness to offer to accomplish at one leap what science will not promise until next year or the year after. The whole thing was a failure — worse than a failure: a fiasco. That cancerous wall at Roche, if it still stands, is a kind of ultimate cairn where the only member of the farthest, craziest expedition buried himself from the arctic wolves and the weasels with his last will and testament in his hand: "Il faut être absolument moderne."

Perhaps. But if one rejects the pretension of Rimbaud one is left with its opposite. If poetry is not a journey toward the Unknown it must be a journey toward the Known and the Known is as difficult to reach — more difficult even, for in the journey toward the Known we can expect no help from our new sister, science. One of the most confident of recent cosmic summaries, Hoyle's *Nature of the Universe*, ends with this sentence: "Perhaps the most majestic feature of our whole existence is that while our intelligences are powerful enough to penetrate deeply into the evolution of this quite incredible Universe, we still have not the smallest clue to our own fate."

It is our own fate, of course, which every poem looks for — if not beyond the starry archipelagos in those regions which modern cosmologists call "unknowable," then nearer by, under the lintel of a Lesbos door when the moon has gone down and the Pleiades, or among the fading daffodils on an English morning, or with a girl's body in one's arms — O my America. We may say what we wish about the presumption of Rimbaud but the same things or worse must be said of more modest poets. They too are presumptuous. They may not pretend to fetch the fire from heaven but they do pretend to find, in the familiar world, signatures and indications which science has not found and which philosophy has never seen however it may talk about them. Indeed it is precisely this pretension which leads us to use the word *great* of certain poets and their work.

Greatness in poetry does not refer to the dimensions of the work or the skill with which it is accomplished or even to the fame it earns. There is poetry in English as in other tongues which displays the most astonishing virtuosity and achieves the most impressive effects without being thought of, for that reason, as great; and there are poets — the best-read contemporaries of almost any generation — whose repute is fabulous and world-wide but whose greatness is merely a matter of journalistic convenience. What distinguishes Homer and Shakespeare is not only their extravagant gifts as masters of words and makers of images but what we call, inadequately enough, their "universality," meaning their inexplicable ability to hold together in a single form the contradictions and perversities of the familiar world — those "extremities," between which, as Yeats puts it in "Vacillation," "Man runs his course." When Yeats, in a strophe of that same poem, brings day and night, life and death, together in an image rooted in the common human heart he is boasting of the power of poetry in words as outrageous as any Rimbaud ever used:

> *From man's blood-sodden heart are sprung*
> *Those branches of the night and day*
> *Where the gaudy moon is hung.*
> *What's the meaning of all song?*
> *"Let all things pass away."*

The only difference is that the power claimed for poetry here is a power over the familiar, not the visionary.

To think, therefore, as we like to do in our newly limitless universe, of the "limits" of poetry, we must think not only of the cairn at the end of Rimbaud's disastrous expedition to the Unknown but of a famous and mawkish stone in that part of the protestant cemetery in Rome nearest the pyramid of Caius Cestius, which reads: "This grave contains all that was mortal of a young English poet who on his death bed in the bitterness of his heart at the malicious power of his enemies desired these words to be engraven on his tomb stone 'Here lies one whose name was writ in water' February 24, 1821." Did the journey of John Keats to what he called the "wide arable land of events," the familiar human world, end as disastrously as Rimbaud's expedition toward the millions of gold birds? Is that embarrassing Roman stone a confession of failure too, and do the pretensions of the most human poetry collapse with the pretensions of the most inhuman, leaving only a grave here and a wall there?

For there can be no question but that John Keats, for all the brevity of his life and the abbreviation of his work, was a great poet precisely in the most human sense. He has been listed so long as a Romantic and discussed so frequently as a member of that school that his true dimensions have been obscured even while his reputation has grown. In the narrow definition of the term he is not a Romantic at all. His humanity is at once so human and so broad that it can be compared only with Shakespeare's and he was committed, no less than Shakespeare, to that labor of the discovery of the wholeness of our destiny as men which is the measure of a universal poet. His contemporaries, those who defended him as well as those who attacked him, thought of him, of course, in other terms, as did the Victorians and the nineteenth-century critics in general. As David Perkins puts it in his *Quest for Permanence:* "Many nineteenth-century critics, stressing the sensuous relish and mazy enchantment of Keats's verse, felt that he lacked what Arnold called 'the matured power of moral interpretation,' " and even Yeats, who formed his literary estimates in the London of the nineties, has Ille, in "Ego Dominus Tuus," describe Keats as a schoolboy

> *With face and nose pressed to a sweet-shop window,*
> *For certainly he sank into his grave*
> *His senses and his heart unsatisfied,*
> *And made — being poor, ailing and ignorant,*
> *Shut out from all the luxury of the world,*
> *The coarse-bred son of a livery-stable keeper —*
> *Luxuriant song.*

It was not only the sweets in the sweet-shop window John Keats saw. And his power of moral interpretation was considerably more mature in his early twenties than that of the middle-aged Victorians who thought he lacked it. It was John Keats, not Arnold, who saw past the laughing eye of Bobby Burns to the sad man under: "His misery is a dead weight . . . He talked with bitches — he drank with blackguards — he was miserable. We can see horribly clear in the works of such a man his whole life, as if we were God's spies." And it was Keats, not the nineteenth-century critics who put him down as a sensualist and escapist, to whom a young girl's happiness — even the happiness of his brother's bride — was a frightening thing: "Women must want imagination and they may thank God for it; and so may we that a delicate being can feel happy without any sense of crime. It puzzles me, and I have no sense of logic to comfort me . . ." When one considers that Keats was not a Calvinist — he was in fact an agnostic — one understands that the words mean exactly what they say. They were written by the same man who could declare: "Were it in my choice I would reject a Petrarchal crown on account of my dying day and because women have cancers."

The fact is that Keats had a truer sense of the tragic than any English poet since Shakespeare and precisely because he took a sharper delight in the loveliness of the world. We are snobs of the tragic in our century. We believe that because we are the first to accept and even to relish the meaninglessness of human life we are also the first to comprehend the human tragedy. But in truth we are among the last, for the tragic, like everything else in man's experience, comes wholly alive only in the presence of its opposite. Our modern disillusioned hero who faces the absurdity of the world with an ironic eye and refuses to kill himself, not because he wishes to live, but because his persistence in that meaningless confrontation gives him a sense of stoical nobility, is not a tragic figure. To taste the human tragedy one must taste at the same time the possibility of human happiness, for it is only when the two are known together in a single knowledge that either can be known.

This Keats understood from the beginning of his brief life as a poet and it was through this understanding that his journey toward the Known was made. The statement of faith is found in many poems but most explicitly in the "Ode on Melancholy" which is actually not at all the poem suggested by its title but a definition rather of what we would call the tragic sense. Melancholy, in the ode, is not that moody mopishness the word evokes for us. It is not, that is to say, a state of mind to be cured as soon as possible or drugged or drowned in oblivion, temporary or permanent:

> *No, no! go not to Lethe, neither twist*
> *Wolf's-bane, tight-rooted, for its poisonous wine;*
> *Nor suffer thy pale forehead to be kiss'd*
>   *By nightshade, ruby grape of Proserpine . . .*

On the contrary melancholy is a mystery of sorrow, a "wakeful anguish of the soul," to be experienced to the full:

> *. . . when the melancholy fit shall fall*
>   *Sudden from heaven like a weeping cloud . . .*
> *Then glut thy sorrow . . .*

And this sorrow can be glutted only upon its opposite — on the lovely transience of the world, the transient loveliness:

>   *. . . on a morning rose,*
> *Or on the rainbow of the salt-sand wave,*
>   *Or on the wealth of globèd peonies;*
> *Or if thy mistress some rich anger shows,*

Emprison her soft hand, and let her rave,
And feed deep, deep upon her peerless eyes.

It can be glutted only among its opposites because it is *there*
that this wakeful anguish of the soul exists: it *"dwells* with
Beauty" —

> . . . *Beauty that must die;*
> *And Joy, whose hand is ever at his lips*
> *Bidding adieu; and aching Pleasure nigh,*
> *Turning to poison while the bee-mouth sips:*
> *Aye, in the very temple of Delight*
> *Veil'd Melancholy has her sovran shrine . . .*

And the only man who can truly know this Melancholy, the
only man who can "taste the sadness of her might, / And be
among her cloudy trophies hung," is the man who is capable
of her opposite, capable of delight, strong enough to dare
delight. Her sovran shrine is

> . . . *seen of none save him whose strenuous tongue*
> *Can burst Joy's grape against his palate fine . . .*

Our generation is fond of quoting Yeats's remark that
it is not until a man comes to understand that life is a
tragedy that his life truly begins. What Keats is saying in
the "Ode on Melancholy" is something more, something the
sensibility of our time forgets: that no man comes to under-
stand that life is a tragedy — no man earns the tragic sense
— until he dares to taste and love what death will take away.

But the "Ode on Melancholy" is rather a point of departure
than a stage of arrival in that journey toward the Known
to which Keats was committed. It is in the two great odes,

the "Ode to a Nightingale" and the "Ode on a Grecian Urn,"
that the boldness of the undertaking can be measured and its
success or failure judged, for these two poems are not state-
ments *about* the contradictions of our human experi-
ence; they are not assertions, as the "Ode on Melancholy"
is, that the opposites are one; they are *discoveries* of that
oneness.

The "Ode to a Nightingale" begins in the "old rag and
bone shop of the heart" where all things mortal must: in a
common mortal experience. There is a bird singing and a
man listening — a bird singing so beautifully as almost to
seem free of time and place, and a man listening from his place
in time. There is a nightingale. And there is the one who hears
it. It is a meeting most of us have known and though the words
in which it is described are not words available to us or even
words we would choose ourselves — the vocabulary of any
language changes in a century and a half — nevertheless we
understand them. We have all been trapped awake at one
time or another, most often in our youth, by some aspect of
this earth we live in — by what we call, knowing and still not
altogether knowing what we mean, its "beauty." And we
have all felt what the listener of the ode feels whether we
would confess it to ourselves or not.

> My heart aches, and a drowsy numbness pains
>   My sense, as though of hemlock I had drunk,
> Or emptied some dull opiate to the drains
>   One minute past, and Lethe-wards had sunk:
> 'Tis not through envy of thy happy lot,
>   But being too happy in thine happiness, —
>   That thou, light-wingèd Dryad of the trees,
>   In some melodious plot
>   Of beechen green, and shadows numberless,
>   Singest of summer in full-throated ease.

To come upon some moment of the loveliness of the earth wide awake to it, naked to it, is in fact to fall too far into happiness, and to fall too far into happiness is to feel the touch of pain. All this is part of what we know together about our lives and can recall, but in Keats's ode it is not recalled: it happens — happens in the words themselves — the shape they make of sound and meaning.

But there is also something more in our common experience of the meeting with the nightingale. There is not only the heartache which the moment of loveliness can cause but a longing, which is part of it, to

> . . . *leave the world unseen,*
> *And with thee fade away into the forest dim:*

> *Fade far away, dissolve, and quite forget*
> *What thou among the leaves hast never known,*
> *The weariness, the fever, and the fret*
> *Here, where men sit and hear each other groan;*
> *Where palsy shakes a few, sad, last gray hairs,*
> *Where youth grows pale, and spectre-thin, and dies;*
> *Where but to think is to be full of sorrow*
> *And leaden-eyed despairs . . .*

Beauty, although it is the world which shows it to us — half shows it to us — has a strangeness about it which places it against the world, beyond the world, so that our love of it, our longing for it — perhaps the most poignant of our human longings — is itself a contradiction: to come to the nightingale we must leave our mortal world and even, it may be, our mortal selves behind us.

It is in this contradiction that the "Ode to a Nightingale" finds its spring and the force that drives it. With Keats, as with all great, true poets, a poem is not the perfected expression of a predetermined thought but is itself the process of its thinking moving from perception to perception, sense to sense; and in none of Keats's poems is the living process more alive than it is here. The ode begins at the moment of meeting of man and song, at the point of paradox. It proceeds to a pursuit of the song, but a pursuit which is at first more nearly escape from the unlovely world than search for the unseen singer — an escape by the oldest means of mortal evasion:

> *O for a draught of vintage! that hath been*
> *Cool'd a long age in the deep-delvèd earth . . .*
> *O for a beaker full of the warm South . . .*
> *That I might drink, and leave the world unseen,*
> *And with thee fade away . . .*

an escape which loses itself almost at once in the realization that the evasion of the world and the achievement of the nightingale are not the same. One may and briefly does forget one's troubles with a draught of vintage — forget the misery and suffering of a world where young Tom Keats could grow pale and spectre-thin and die — but one does not and cannot fly at one's desire even with a beaker full of the warm South. In the meeting with the nightingale the leopards of intoxication will not suffice. And so the pursuit begins again — this time on a thrust, a cast, of the imagination:

> *Away! away! for I will fly to thee,*
> *Not charioted by Bacchus and his pards,*
> *But on the viewless wings of Poesy . . .*

And the cast succeeds or seems to:

> *Already with thee! tender is the night . . .*

Listener and bird have met in the beech wood of the imagination where nothing can be seen by sight, that "angel of consecutive reasoning" — where everything must be sensed or guessed at:

> . . . here there is no light,
> Save what from heaven is with the breezes blown
> Through verdurous glooms and winding mossy ways.

It is by their fragrance that grass and thicket and hawthorn are discerned and there are even flowers here in the freedom of this imagined dark whose season has not come:

> I cannot see what flowers are at my feet,
> Nor what soft incense hangs upon the boughs,
> But, in embalmèd darkness, guess each sweet
> Wherewith the seasonable month endows
> The grass, the thicket and the fruit-tree wild;
> White hawthorn, and the pastoral eglantine;
> Fast-fading violets cover'd up in leaves;
> And mid-May's eldest child,
> The coming musk-rose, full of dewy wine,
> The murmurous haunt of flies on summer eves.

But though the imagination has made its way to the embalmèd darkness where the nightingale sings and though the world with all its fever and its fret is far, far behind — so far as to be lost — the pursuit has not yet ended. There is still the bird singing and the listener listening — "thou" and "I." The song itself has not been taken, is not possessed: the longed-for beauty is not *mine*. And why? Because the listener's self, the listener's identity, is still between.

It is this last obstacle which always stands between the lover and the loveliness he longs for, the loveliness he never

will possess however he may speak of its "possession." And it
is this last obstacle which breaks the poem off again — breaks
off the difficult pursuit:

> *Darkling I listen; and, for many a time*
> *I have been half in love with easeful Death . . .*

The listener listens but it is not the song he thinks of. It is
death, the dissolution of identity:

> *Now more than ever seems it rich to die,*
> *To cease upon the midnight with no pain,*
> *While thou art pouring forth thy soul abroad*
> *In such an ecstasy! . . .*

And so the long pursuit begins again. If the imagination has
failed in its triumph as the leopards of intoxication also failed,
then death is perhaps the only conqueror of the contradiction
at the heart of the desire for beauty: "To cease upon the mid-
night with no pain, / While thou art pouring forth thy soul
abroad . . ."

But this third cast fails before it has begun. To die to one's
self is to die to the song also — to die *to* it, not *into* it:

> *Still wouldst thou sing, and I have ears in vain —*
> *To thy high requiem become a sod.*

And with the failure comes a realization of the nature of this
song which has so drawn the listener — a realization which
many men before John Keats had come to in the presence of
the beauty of the world but none with so strong and sure an
apprehension. *This song can never be possessed either in
space and time or out of it.* It cannot be possessed beyond the
limits of space and time because the listener cannot be there to
possess it. It cannot be possessed within those limits because

what draws the listener is not within the mortal world — that lasting loveliness it seems to promise:

> *Thou wast not born for death, immortal Bird!*

Every well-wrought play, Maxwell Anderson once observed, has a scene in which the hero recognizes his predicament and faces it. This is the recognition scene in the drama of the "Ode to a Nightingale." It is not, the listener now understands, the small bird of the beech wood or its little trill of song which has drawn him. Rather it is Song itself, immortal Song which the hungry generations cannot trample down, which emperors have listened to and peasants, which the human heart has always heard:

> *Thou wast not born for death, immortal Bird!*
> *No hungry generations tread thee down;*
> *The voice I hear this passing night was heard*
> *In ancient days by emperor and clown:*
> *Perhaps the self-same song that found a path*
> *Through the sad heart of Ruth, when, sick for home,*
> *She stood in tears amid the alien corn . . .*

But the moment of recognition does not end with the figure of Ruth. It is not only the song itself the listener has recognized: it is also the true nature of this pursuit of his which follows it. For if the bird can never be reached nor its song possessed then the effort to reach the one and possess the other is a delusion — a delusion which can tempt a man too far beyond this mortal world where all the lives are lived. That "voice I hear this passing night" may be

> *The same that oft-times hath*
> *Charm'd magic casements, opening on the foam*
> *Of perilous seas, in faery lands forlorn.*

There are readers who think of the world these lines describe as a world of fairy wildness and beauty, a world to be desired, but they are wrong. What does *perilous* mean but full of peril? And what is *forlorn* in its true sense, the sense in which Milton used it, but desolate, forsaken and abandoned — forsaken by humankind, abandoned by men? And what are these "faery lands"? Are they the fairyland of *A Midsummer Night's Dream* or are they that country of the enchanted and the lost which the knight-at-arms in Keats's own "La Belle Dame Sans Merci" had visited with the faery's child — that country where he dreamed he saw "pale kings and princes too, / Pale warriors, death pale were they all" — where he dreamed "their starved lips in the gloam / With horrid warning gapèd wide"?

The ode itself leaves no doubt as to the meaning of these lines for it is the word *forlorn*, twice repeated, which breaks off the whole pursuit and brings the poem to its close. What was at first the song of the actual bird singing "of summer in full-throated ease" and then the song of the imagined bird "pouring forth thy soul abroad / In such an ecstasy" and then the song of the "immortal Bird" which men have known from the beginning of their history becomes now a siren song that can lure men's hearts beyond the world of men altogether to a beautiful and dreadful world of perilous seas streaked with grey driven foam in faery lands where no men are. It is, indeed, to this ultimate recognition of the danger of the pursuit of the song too long and too far that the repetition of the word is due. Robert Bridges thought the repetition was a weakness: "... the introduction of the last stanza is artificial." But surely he was mistaken. It has happened to all of us to hear in our own mouths a word the full meaning of which is not understood until it is spoken, and so to speak it twice. Yeats, in "The Second Coming," repeats, in this way, the words which supplied his title, and Keats, in the same way and for the same reason, repeats here the word forlorn. It teaches him his meaning:

> *. . . forlorn.*
>
> *Forlorn!   the very word is like a bell*
> *To toll me back from thee to my sole self!*

It had been *from* himself — to lose himself in that too happy song — that the listener had first set out. It had been from himself, by losing himself in his own cessation, that he had hoped to reach the song turned ecstasy. It is *to* himself that he comes back, the dangerous pursuit abandoned. And it is that repeated word that sends him back and so provides the hinge that turns pursuit and poem on themselves. With the word forlorn, the iron tolling of that bell, the hunt is over, the *chasse spirituelle* is ended, and the imagination is whistled home as "fancy":

> *. . . the fancy cannot cheat so well*
> *As she is fam'd to do, deceiving elf . . .*

Everything has changed. The song has become a "plaintive anthem." The Bird is bird again and drifts away across familiar fields:

> *Past the near meadows, over the still stream,*
> *Up the hill-side . . .*

until its singing is

> *. . . buried deep*
> *In the next valley-glades . . .*

Even the longing and the pain have become unreal.

Was it a vision, or a waking dream?
Fled is that music: — do I wake or sleep?

What has happened is that a word spoken first to describe that world beyond the world to which the pursuit of the nightingale can tempt us has become, in the speaking of it, a judgment upon that world and upon the pursuit which can carry the listener so far. The imagination, precisely because it has this power to lead us beyond the human world, can be dangerous as Rimbaud learned and as Yeats learned later. It can be dangerous not only to imaginative men but even to the man who lives by the imagination, the poet himself, for if he follows it too far beyond the human world he will be poet no longer but a dreamer only. John Keats did not need, as Rimbaud did, to leave the art of poetry to learn this. He did not need to wait and see as Yeats did. He learned it for himself in the writing of this poem which returns at the end, and willingly returns, to "my sole self."

Adieu! the fancy cannot cheat so well
As she is fam'd to do . . .

Those critics of the "Ode to a Nightingale" who read it as the account of a search for visionary illumination ending in failure surely mistake its structure and its tone. The tragedy of the ode is not an aesthetic tragedy private to its author. It is a universal tragedy common to all men. If the song is not possessed in the poem it is because it cannot be possessed in the world of human experience in which one can neither lose oneself alive into the beauty one loves, nor lose oneself into it in death, nor follow it beyond the world where no self can be. And the return to the sole self at the poem's end is not the return of failure and defeat. It is the return of realization — of that which *makes* real. It is to the sole self we must all return either to live or die, for we die in the sole self and it is in the sole self we begin to live. Keats, as we know from the journal letter to his brother and sister-in-law, had little sympathy with the common Christian notion that life on earth is justified by a hoped-for escape to life in heaven. Life on earth, unhappy as it is, was justified to Keats in and of itself, for it was here, he said, in this "vale of soul-making" that a self, an identity, is achieved. To return to that identity from the pursuit of the nightingale's song to the world's end and beyond is not, therefore, to confess defeat but to affirm the integrity of the human self. If the nightingale is never seen nor the song possessed, still the listener stands there.

Such a resolution may not resolve the longing which set the poem in motion but it is a resolution notwithstanding, for it brings that longing face to face with the paradox it is — the paradox of the listener and the song — of beauty and the beholder of the beautiful who cannot take what he most longs for. This is the deepest contradiction of our human consciousness which, if it could lose itself as it desires in what it loves, would no longer love — nor be. The "Ode to a Nightingale" leaves the paradox intact, as life still leaves it, but it brings it closer to our senses than it had ever been before.

The essential difference between this poem and the "Ode on a Grecian Urn" is here — in the dramatic resolution. The human situation in both poems is much the same — a paradoxical situation which, in the "Grecian Urn," brings the most fleeting of all passions face to face with the permanence for which passion yearns, and turns the one into the other: the figures on the urn are men and gods and maidens in "mad pursuit," in "struggle to escape" — but they are also motionless actors in an eternity of stone. Moreover, the progression of the poem is much the same as the progression of the "Ode to a Nightingale." That is to say that a drama of perceptions is played out in both poems and that, in both, a "recognition scene" turns and resolves the action. But the resolution of the "Ode on a Grecian Urn" is very different from the image of the sole and single self which hears the fading of the nightingale's "plaintive anthem." The "Ode on a Grecian Urn" ends with a *statement* — one of the most famous and one of the most hotly debated statements in English literature:

> *Beauty is truth, truth beauty, — that is all*
> *Ye know on earth, and all ye need to know.*

The variety of opinions on these eighteen words is extraordinary. Sir Arthur Quiller-Couch, the editor of the once-admired *Oxford Book of English Verse*, examines them as the expression of an abstract proposition and takes his critical position solidly in dissent: "To put it solidly," he protests, "that is a vague observation: to anyone whom life has taught to face facts and define his terms, actually an uneducated conclusion, albeit pardonable in one so young . . ." Mr. T. S. Eliot, one of the most highly regarded critics of this century, goes even farther. The statement made by these words, he writes, "seems to me meaningless: or perhaps the fact that it is grammatically meaningless conceals another meaning from me." In what way the statement is "grammatically meaningless" is not explained but Mr. Eliot defines his terms by contrasting Keats's sentence with Shakespeare's "ripeness is all" which has "profound emotional meaning with at least no literal fallacy" and with Dante's "la sua voluntade è

nostra pace" which, says Mr. Eliot, is *literally* true. Mr.
Eliot, however, was preceded as dominant British critic by
another distinguished poet whose view of Keats's statement
was equally definite and quite opposed. Robert Bridges was
no admirer of the ode as a whole, which seemed to him
"unprogressive" and "monotonous" and "scattered," with
the result that the effect is one of "poverty in spite of the
beauty" until you come to the last lines. The last lines,
however, are "very fine and make a sort of recovery with
their forcible directness."

With the authorities divided in this way about the merits
of Keats's statement as statement it becomes obvious that
no progress can be made by abstracting the resolution of the
ode from the poem or contrasting the two. The "statement"
must be read *in* the poem. The question is not whether
beauty is in fact truth and truth in fact beauty. The question
is how this curious equation which interchanges beauty and
truth and makes their equality, not to say their identity with
each other, the sum of necessary earthly knowledge relates
to the poem itself.

But what is the poem itself? Its subject is, of course, as
its title indicates, a Grecian urn: an "Attic shape" with
"marble men and maidens overwrought." But is the poem
simply a description of that Attic shape, seen perhaps in some
museum two thousand years after it was made?

> *Thou still unravish'd bride of quietness,*
> *Thou foster-child of Silence and slow Time,*
> *Sylvan historian . . .*

Whatever else this is, it is not description: Still unravished
bride: bride, but still to be one. The urn, it seems, old as
it is, is somehow pristine still. It is not a relic left behind

by time, and surrounded now by the silence which seems to set apart all ancient works of art. It is the foster-child of time and silence — something *fostered* by them, cared for by them — and still childlike. Everthing said about the urn is paradoxical. It is untouched by the quietness that holds it still and yet it is held by that motionlessness, that "quietness," as intimately as a bride. It has lived with silence and slow time and yet it is young.

And what is true of the words as meanings is even truer of the words as sounds. Nowhere in English poetry is there a lovelier, more alluring cadence than the cadence of those first twelve beats. The slow-pacing meter and the sliding syllables are all seduction. But nowhere either are there sounds more timeless and eternal than those five long echoes of the letter *i*.

It is perhaps the sound more than the meaning that reveals the nature of the paradox the urn expresses. The contradiction is the contradiction of eternity and present — the "eternal present" of the work of art — that paradox our human hearts imagine but which nature does not know. It is this paradox which provides the poignance of those first two lines. And it is this paradox which becomes explicit as the ode draws nearer to the urn and sees its "marble men and maidens" closer to. If the urn were merely a Grecian urn, these figures would belong to the past of Greek antiquity and no questions would need be asked them. They would be *then*, not *now*. But because the urn is what it is, they are *both* then and now.

> *What leaf-fringed legend haunts about thy shape*
> *Of deities or mortals, or of both,*
>   *In Tempe or the dales of Arcady?*
> *What men or gods are these? what maidens loth?*
> *What mad pursuit? What struggle to escape?*
>   *What pipes and timbrels? What wild ecstasy?*

The place may be Tempe or the dales of Arcady but the legend is no legend of the past. It is a legend which has for subject what all life has for passionate subject always. These men and women live in an eternity which is also the intensest *now*. The imagination which has trapped them in its cage of form has trapped them there alive —

> *For ever warm and still to be enjoy'd,*
> *For ever panting, and for ever young . . .*

It is that "for ever panting" which reveals the tragic shadow of the contradiction. These vivid and desiring figures can never reach the end of their desire, for the eternal present of the urn can never change. It can never become another later and fulfilling present:

> *Fair youth, beneath the trees, thou canst not leave*
> *Thy song, nor ever can those trees be bare;*
> *Bold lover, never, never canst thou kiss,*
> *Though winning near the goal . . .*

But, to the ode, this tragedy does not matter. Or at least it is the lesser of the two tragedies. Life on the urn — that eternal present of about-to-be which the imagination has conceived — is richer than our mortal life of fulfillment and defeat:

> *. . . yet, do not grieve;*
> *She cannot fade, though thou hast not thy bliss,*
> *For ever wilt thou love, and she be fair!*

Here, one would think, the impulse of the ode had spent itself. The paradox of the world of art, the world of the imagination, has been given shape and form. The contradiction implicit in that world has been admitted. The imagination has been defended notwithstanding the defect. The "thought" which Robert Bridges ascribed to the ode — that "ideal art" is superior to nature "because of its unchanging expression of perfection" — has been spelled out in full and demonstrated with the line, "For ever wilt thou love and she be fair." Why then does not the poem end?

But it does not end. The ode goes on to repeat its affirmation and to repeat it, furthermore, with an insistence which does not strengthen our belief:

> *Ah, happy, happy boughs! that cannot shed*
> *Your leaves, nor ever bid the Spring adieu;*
> *And, happy melodist, unwearièd,*
> *For ever piping songs for ever new;*
> *More happy love! more happy, happy love!*
> *For ever warm and still to be enjoy'd,*
> *For ever panting, and for ever young;*
> *All breathing human passion far above,*
> *That leaves a heart high-sorrowful and cloy'd,*
> *A burning forehead, and a parching tongue.*

Why this insistence? Why this excess of "happiness"? It seems unlikely that John Keats, whose sensibility was at least as perceptive as ours, did not hear what we hear in those too protesting lines. And it seems even more unlikely that a poet as much master of his means as Keats should not have intended the consequences of a repetition as persistent and excessive as that of the word *happy* here. To us, reading the lines, these boughs and melodists and lovers who are six times happy because they can never live the season's end or the song's end or the love's are perhaps too happy, and life in the eternity of the imagination is, in consequence, less perfect than they think. But if it occurs to us to feel this because of the construction of the lines is it not perhaps because the lines are so constructed that we cannot help but feel it? And is it not possible that the contrast between this excessive happiness and the "breathing human passion" of the cloyed heart and the parching tongue is intended also?

Certainly in a poem by Keats it is possible. And in the "Ode on a Grecian Urn" it is certain. For it is with this confrontation that the tone of the ode changes and the theme with it:

> *Who are these coming to the sacrifice?*
> *To what green altar, O mysterious priest,*
> *Lead'st thou that heifer lowing at the skies,*
> *And all her silken flanks with garlands drest?*
> *What little town by river or sea shore,*
> *Or mountain-built with peaceful citadel,*
> *Is emptied of this folk, this pious morn? . . .*

The ode here has left the urn, for the town is not represented on the urn. We cannot tell where it is, whether on a mountain somewhere or by a river or near the sea — questions which would have answered themselves if the town were visible. It is only the people *from* the town who are in the legend where nothing changes — where the lover can never have his love. But, unlike the lover, these pious worshippers have no certainty of eternal bliss. Their certainty is different, and so too is the eternal certainty of their town:

> *And, little town, thy streets for evermore*
> *Will silent be; and not a soul to tell*
> *Why thou art desolate, can e'er return.*

This is the moment of recognition in the "Ode on a Grecian Urn" as the repetition of the word "forlorn" was the moment of recognition in the "Ode to a Nightingale." To fill the zone of the urn with these figures in their forever of about-to-be, some human habitation somewhere upon this changing earth has had to be emptied of its mortal folk. There is, that is to say, a human price to be paid for the eternal present the imagination can create. There is a relationship between that price and the paradox of the unravished bride. But what relationship?

It is to that question the poem, in its last stanza, turns. The tone now is sober and direct. The urn is no longer that forever panting moment delighting in its contradictions. It is a "shape," a "form," — in brief, a work of art. And its figures are no longer figures in that eternal passion, that enchanted dance of never yet. They are "marble men and maidens" who exist not in a "legend" but a "brede," a border — neither in past or present but in stone. And as for eternity, the only part this changed urn has in that is its ability — the ability of any work of art — to "tease us out of thought" — to draw us past the reach of thought to follow:

> O Attic shape! Fair attitude! with brede
>   Of marble men and maidens overwrought,
> With forest branches and the trodden weed;
>   Thou, silent form, dost tease us out of thought
> As doth eternity: Cold Pastoral!
>   When old age shall this generation waste,
>   Thou shalt remain, in midst of other woe
>   Than ours, a friend to man, to whom thou say'st . . .

And it is here that the two lines fall which have so divided the opinions. What the urn, returned to itself, brought back

to "shape," to "form," its figures marble, has to say to man
is this [1]:

> *Beauty is truth, truth beauty, — that is all*
> *Ye know on earth, and all ye need to know.*

If this is the resolution of the poem — and it is clearly
presented as the resolution — then it must resolve that con-
tradictory relationship between the unending happiness and
the desolate town which stands before it. But what have
"truth" and "beauty" to do with these? Well, what *is*
"beauty" in the ode? Is it not the "flowery tale," the
"leaf-fringed legend" of those eternally desirous lovers?
And if "beauty" in the ode is that eternity, is not "truth" its
opposite: the "truth" of the little town emptied of its folk to
fill the unchanging legend of the urn? I should say it was.
I should say "truth" in the ode is the order existing in time:
"beauty" in the ode is the order imposed by the imagination.
Both have been there from the beginning of the action, set over
against each other in a contradiction which has created, indeed,
the whole spring and stress of the poem.

But how is this contradiction resolved in the curious saying
which equates truth and beauty with each other — iden-
tifies them with each other? It is understandable, perhaps,
that beauty, meaning the order imposed by the imagination,
should be truth, meaning the truth of the world of time.
We know, from the famous passage in the letter to Bailey,
that Keats thought it was: "I am certain of nothing but of
the holiness of the heart's affections and the truth of imagi-
nation. What the imagination seizes as beauty must be truth."

----

[1] I follow Douglas Bush in believing that the urn speaks the whole of the
two lines, not only because Professor Bush is here the golden authority but
because he seems to me to have the best of the argument.

And we know, from the ode itself, what he meant, for the ode, in its first stanzas, has in fact seized upon beauty and *made* it true — true in the world of time. It has stopped and held passion, pursuit, music, even the leafing of the trees — stopped them *as they are* and held them under the aspect of eternity, compelling us to see, not by telling us but by show- ing us, that, so stopped, so held, this image of life is true to *life:* that love, forever unrealized, *is* still love — not idealized love but "breathing, panting love." Beauty, which is to say the order imposed by the imagination, has not merely been *said* in the ode to be truth, meaning the order existing in time, it has *become* truth in and for the poem. The imagi- nation, which is the one weapon men possess in their struggle with time and their own mortality — the flowing away of the world — has proved itself as powerful as time. It has turned to truth the beauty it has seized.

But if this justifies the first half of the equation what, then, does the second mean? Why could not the statement have been left as it stood in the letter to Bailey? This question we can, I think, answer from the ode itself. The statement could not be left as it was because there is a price one pays for the exercise of this power of the imagination to turn beauty to truth: there is the desolate town. To live only in the imagination, only in the eternal present which the imagination can impose upon the flowing away of time, is to abandon and leave deserted the human world. A second term must therefore be included if the equation is to hold. The power of the mortal world over the imagination must be accepted by and for the imagination in the same breath in which one affirms the power of the imagination over the mortal world. The "beauty" of time — of experience — of what Keats called "circumstance" — of the "arable field of events" — must be accepted in the same breath in which one asserts the "truth" of those eternities the imagination can preserve from time and circumstance. If this can be done the equation will complete itself and become whole. One will no longer assert only that what the imagination seizes upon as beauty must be truth. One will say also that what time presents as truth must be accepted in the imagination as beauty — the beauty of that circumstance in which Keats declared the identity of a man is formed.

Mr. Eliot, as I have remarked, disparages Keats's "statement" by comparing it with Dante's "In His will is our peace." To me Keats's words have meaning in the selfsame sense. The promise of the "Ode on a Grecian Urn" is not, it is true, peace of mind: the human "woe" will remain as long as men do. But there is a promise notwithstanding — the promise that the woe can be confronted by the man who is able to accept the beauty of the whole of truth and the wholeness of the truth of beauty. The ultimate meaning of which poetry is capable seems to me to beckon in those lines. "What is the meaning of all song?" Yeats asks himself, and answers, "Let all things pass away." To face the truth of the passing away of the world and make song of it, make beauty of it, is not to solve the riddle of our mortal lives but perhaps to accomplish something more.

Index of Names and Titles

"A la Musique" (Rimbaud), 159–60

"A Une Raison" (Rimbaud), 168, 171

"Après le Déluge" (Rimbaud), 169, 170–71

Aristotle, 81, 82, 83

"Artificial Paradises" (Baudelaire), 157

"Au Cabaret Vert" (Rimbaud), 160

Bardey, Alfred, 163

"Bateau Ivre" (Rimbaud), 154–57, 163

Baudelaire, Charles, 69, 70, 83, 110–11, 157

Beardsley, Aubrey, 134

"Belle Dame Sans Merci, La" (Keats), 186

Biographia Literaria (Coleridge), 42

Blake, William, 93

Book of Odes (Confucius), 49, 60

"Bridge at Ten Shin" (Li Po), 59

Bridges, Robert, 186, 194

Camus, Albert, 150

"Carcass, A" (Baudelaire), 70–71

Cézanne, Paul, 70

"Chant de Guerre Parisien" (Rimbaud), 152

"Charogne, Une" (Baudelaire), 70–71

Claudel, Paul, 171

"Cloud, The" (Shelley), 22

Coleridge, Samuel Taylor, 42, 46, 63, 78–79, 80

Colum, Mary, 128

Confucius, 60

"Congo, The" (Lindsay), 44–45

Cowley, Malcolm, 119–20, 122, 137, 138

Cruikshank, John, 172
Cummings, E. E., 119, 137

"Daniel" (Lindsay), 45
Dante Alighieri, 9, 115
Degas, Hilaire, 14, 22, 24
Demeny, Paul, 152, 153
Dickinson, Edward, 103
Dickinson, Emily, 72, 91–114
Dirac, Paul Adrien Maurice, 37
"Dirge" (Webster), 23
Divine Comedy (Dante), 9
"Do Not Go Gentle Into That Good Night" (Thomas), 10
Donne, John, 73, 105
Dowson, Ernest, 134

"Easter 1916" (Yeats), 141–44
"Ego Dominus Tuus" (Yeats), 176
Eliot, T. S., 190–91, 199
Ellman, Richard, 19
Enormous Room, The (Cummings), 120

Fang, Achilles, 4
"Fêtes de la Faim" (Rimbaud), 166
Finnegan's Wake (Joyce), 16, 18, 19
Frost, Robert, 28, 101
Fu. *See* Wen Fu

Gonne, Maud, 120, 122
Goya, Francisco, 119
Graves, Robert, 45–46
Gregory, Lady, 124, 125
"Grey Rock, The" (Yeats), 133, 139, 140

Herrick, Robert, 23, 30, 36, 37, 38, 41

Hightower, Professor J. R., 50, 51, 53
"Hugh Selwyn Mauberley" (Pound), 30, 39, 135

Illuminations, Les (Rimbaud), 167, 170, 171
"Intimations of Immortality, Ode on the" (Wordsworth), 170
Izambard, Georges, 152, 154, 157, 163

Johnson, Lionel, 131, 134, 135
Johnson, Thomas H., 101
Joyce, James, 16, 18, 19, 123

Keats, John, 7, 42, 173–99
Kelleher, John, 135, 141

"Lake Isle of Innisfree, The" (Yeats), 129
Landor, Walter Savage, 22
Lane, Hugh, 124, 125, 128
LeGallienne, Richard, 134
Lepelletier, 159
Lettres du Voyant (Rimbaud), 151, 156, 159, 161, 163
Lewis, C. Day, 68, 69, 74
"Li Fu-jen" (Emperor Wu-ti), 47
Li Po (Rihaku), 54–60
Lindsay, Vachel, 44, 45
Lu Chi, 4, 6, 7, 8, 9, 22, 44, 47, 149, 171
Lyrical Ballads (Wordsworth, Coleridge), 69

MacNeice, Louis, 123
Mallarmé, Stéphane, 14, 15, 21, 22, 24, 29
Malraux, André, 150

Maritain, Jacques, 151, 164, 170
Marvell, Andrew, 82–88
"Meditation in Time of Civil War" (Yeats), 147
Moore, George, 21, 22

O'Casey, Sean, 123
"Ode on a Grecian Urn" (Keats), 180, 189–99
"Ode to Melancholy" (Keats), 178, 180
"Ode to a Nightingale" (Keats), 180–89, 190, 196
"Ode to the West Wind" (Shelley), 22
"On the Beach at Fontana" (Joyce), 19
On the Boiler (Yeats), 145
"On those that hated 'The Playboy of the Western World' 1907" (Yeats), 123, 129
Oppenheimer, Richard, 37
Oxford Book of English Verse, The, 190

Parnell, Charles Stewart, 126–27
"Pauvres à l'Eglise, Les" (Rimbaud), 151
Payne, Robert, 50, 58
Perkins, David, 176
Playboy of the Western World, The (Synge), 123, 128
Poe, Edgar Allan, 22
"Poëtes de Sept Ans, Les" (Rimbaud), 161
Poetic Image (C. Day Lewis), 68
Poetics (Aristotle), 81
Pomes Penyeach (Joyce), 19
Pound, Ezra, 12, 30, 39, 58, 59, 102

"Première Soirée" (Rimbaud), 159
"Premières Communions, Les" (Rimbaud), 171

Quest for Permanence (Perkins), 176
Quiller-Couch, Sir Arthur, 190

Racine, Jean Baptiste, 153
Read, Sir Herbert, 5
"Relic, The" (Donne), 73
Responsibilities (Yeats), 122, 138
Rhymers Club, The, 134
Richards, Ivor, 37, 38, 74, 80
Rihaku. See Li Po
Rilke, Rainer, 106
Rimbaud, Arthur, 9, 149–72
"Rime of the Ancient Mariner" (Coleridge), 75, 78–79
"Roman" (Rimbaud), 162
Rose, The (Yeats), 131
"Rose of the World, The" (Yeats), 129–30
Ruggles, Eleanor, 45

Sartre, Jean Paul, 150
"Season in Hell, A" (Rimbaud), 164, 172
"Second Coming, The" (Yeats), 77–78, 80, 140, 141, 186
"September 1913" (Yeats), 123, 124–25, 138, 140
Shakespeare, William, 7, 22, 30, 36, 38
Shelley, Percy Bysshe, 22
Snow, C. P., 38
"Song of the Highest Tower" (Rimbaud), 165
"Song of War" (Li Po), 58

Sonnet CXVI (Shakespeare), 33, 38

"Stare's Nest by My Window, The" (Yeats), 147

Starkie, Enid, 157, 158

"Statues, The" (Yeats), 145

Stephen Hero (Joyce), 123

Swinburne, Algernon, 22

Symons, Arthur, 116, 134, 135

Synge, John Millington, 128

"System" (Yeats), 77

T'ang Dynasty, 49, 50, 54

T'ao Yuan-Ming, 56

Tennyson, Alfred Lord, 16, 22

Thomas, Dylan, 10, 11, 12

Tillich, Paul, 75

"To Daffodils" (Herrick), 36, 41

"To a Friend Whose Work" (Yeats), 123, 125–26

"To His Coy Mistress" (Marvell), 61, 82–88

"To Meadows" (Herrick), 23

"To Shade" (Yeats), 123, 126–28, 138

"To a Wealthy Man" (Yeats), 139

Tu Fu, 50, 52

Ulysses (Joyce), 123

"Vacillation" (Yeats), 175

Valade, Léon, 159, 161

"Venus Anadyomène" (Rimbaud), 151

Verlaine, Paul, 158

Waley, Arthur, 47

Webster, John, 23

Wen Fu. *See* Lu Chi

Whalley, George, 79

Wilbur, Richard, 95

Women of Trachis, The (Sophocles), 102

Wordsworth, William, 42, 67, 68, 69, 170

Wu-Ti, Emperor, 47

Yeats, William Butler, 24, 34, 77, 79, 115–47, 175, 199

Yellow Book, The, 134